Trauma-Informed Assessment With Children and Adolescents

Concise Guides on Trauma Care Series

Child Maltreatment: A Developmental Psychopathology Approach
  Kathryn A. Becker-Blease and Patricia K. Kerig

Creating Healing School Communities: School-Based Interventions for Students Exposed to Trauma
  Catherine DeCarlo Santiago, Tali Raviv, and Lisa H. Jaycox

Mental Health Practice With Immigrant and Refugee Youth: A Socioecological Framework
  B. Heidi Ellis, Saida M. Abdi, and Jeffrey P. Winer

Microaggressions and Traumatic Stress: Theory, Research, and Clinical Treatment
  Kevin L. Nadal

Mindfulness-Based Interventions for Trauma and Its Consequences
  David J. Kearney and Tracy L. Simpson

Trauma-Informed Assessment With Children and Adolescents: Strategies to Support Clinicians
  Cassandra Kisiel, Tracy Fehrenbach, Lisa Conradi, and Lindsey Weil

Treating Infants and Young Children Impacted by Trauma: Interventions That Promote Healthy Development
  Joy D. Osofsky, Phillip T. Stepka, and Lucy S. King

Treating PTSD With Cognitive-Behavioral Therapies: Interventions That Work
  Candice M. Monson and Philippe Shnaider

Understanding Elder Abuse: A Clinician's Guide
  Shelly L. Jackson

Trauma-Informed Assessment With Children and Adolescents

Strategies to Support Clinicians

Cassandra Kisiel, Tracy Fehrenbach,
Lisa Conradi, and Lindsey Weil

 AMERICAN PSYCHOLOGICAL ASSOCIATION

Published by
American Psychological Association
750 First Street, NE
Washington, DC 20002
https://www.apa.org

Order Department
https://www.apa.org/pubs/books
order@apa.org

In the U.K., Europe, Africa, and the Middle East, copies may be ordered from Eurospan
https://www.eurospanbookstore.com/apa
info@eurospangroup.com

Typeset in Charter and Interstate by Circle Graphics, Inc., Reisterstown, MD

Printer: Gasch Printing, Odenton, MD
Cover Designer: Beth Schlenoff Design, Bethesda, MD

Library of Congress Cataloging-in-Publication Data

Names: Kisiel, Cassandra, author.
Title: Trauma-informed assessment with children and adolescents : strategies to
  support clinicians / by Cassandra Kisiel [and three others].
Description: Washington, DC : American Psychological Association, [2021] |
  Series: Concise guides on trauma care series | Includes bibliographical references
  and index.
Identifiers: LCCN 2020037960 (print) | LCCN 2020037961 (ebook) |
  ISBN 9781433833854 (paperback) | ISBN 9781433834820 (ebook)
Subjects: LCSH: Psychic trauma in children—Treatment. | Psychic trauma in
  adolescence—Treatment. | Psychodiagnostics.
Classification: LCC RJ506.P66 K57 2021 (print) | LCC RJ506.P66 (ebook) |
  DDC 618.92/8521—dc23
LC record available at https://lccn.loc.gov/2020037960
LC ebook record available at https://lccn.loc.gov/2020037961

https://doi.org/10.1037/0000233-000

Printed in the United States of America

10 9 8 7 6 5 4 3 2 1

Contents

Series Foreword—*Ann T. Chu and Anne P. DePrince*   *vii*

Acknowledgments   *ix*

1. Introduction: Understanding the Rationale for and Benefits
   of Trauma-Informed Assessment   3

2. Key Principles and Essential Organizational Process Elements
   of Trauma-Informed Assessment   17

3. Implementing a Comprehensive Trauma-Informed Assessment   33

4. Tailoring the Trauma-Informed Assessment to the
   Developmental and Sociocultural Context of the Child
   and Family   57

5. Selecting and Integrating Trauma-Informed Assessment
   Tools for Children and Adolescents   85

6. Collaborative and Meaningful Applications of Trauma-
   Informed Assessment   107

7. Conclusions and Future Directions   119

Appendix A: Additional Resources   *127*

Appendix B: Conducting Intakes and Assessments Using Telemental Health *131*

References   *137*

Index   *157*

About the Authors   *169*

Series Foreword

Exposure to traumatic events is all too common, increasing the risk for a range of significant mental problems, such as posttraumatic stress disorder (PTSD) and depression; physical health problems; negative health behaviors, such as smoking and excessive alcohol consumption; impaired social and occupational functioning; and overall lower quality of life. As mass incidents (e.g., September 11, military engagements in Iraq and Afghanistan, natural disasters such as Hurricane Katrina, shootings) have propelled trauma into a brighter public spotlight, the number of trauma survivors seeking services for mental health consequences is increasing. Yet despite the far-ranging consequences of trauma and the high rates of exposure, relatively little emphasis is placed on trauma education in undergraduate and graduate training programs for mental health service providers in the United States. Calls for action have appeared in the American Psychological Association's journal *Psychological Trauma: Theory, Research, Practice, and Policy* with such articles as "The Need for Inclusion of Psychological Trauma in the Professional Curriculum: A Call to Action" by Christine A. Courtois and Steven N. Gold (2009) and "The Art and Science of Trauma-Focused Training and Education" by Anne P. DePrince and Elana Newman (2011). The lack of education in the assessment and treatment of trauma-related distress and associated clinical issues at undergraduate and graduate levels increases the urgency to develop effective trauma resources for students as well as postgraduate professionals.

This book series, Concise Guides on Trauma Care, addresses that urgent need by providing truly translational books that bring the best of trauma psychology science to mental health professions working in diverse settings. To do so, the series focuses on what we know (and do not know) about specific trauma topics, with attention to how trauma psychology science translates to diverse populations (diversity broadly defined, in terms of developmental stage, ethnicity, socioeconomic status, sexual orientation, and so forth).

This series represents one of many efforts undertaken by Division 56 (Trauma Psychology) of the American Psychological Association to advance trauma training and education (e.g., see https://www.apatraumadivision.org/). We are pleased to work with Division 56 and a volunteer editorial board to create this series, which continues to move forward with the publication of this important guide on trauma-informed assessment with children and adolescents by Cassandra Kisiel, Tracy Fehrenbach, Lisa Conradi, and Lindsey Weil. As clinicians, researchers, policy makers, and system leaders seek to better engage children and youth in the assessment process, this monograph offers a practical and accessible guide on the assessment process using a trauma-informed framework. The information provided in this guide will be of great use to mental health professionals in the selection of trauma-informed assessment tools, administration of the tools with engagement of youth and families, adjustments to address sociocultural differences, and integration of the assessment within the treatment process and the broader organizational context. This knowledge will be helpful when working with individuals suffering from a range of trauma-related symptoms, including posttraumatic stress, depression, anxiety, and dissociation. Future books in the series will continue to address a range of assessment, treatment, and developmental issues in trauma-informed care.

—*Ann T. Chu*
Anne P. DePrince
Series Editors

Acknowledgments

We acknowledge with gratitude that this book builds upon more than 2 decades of work in collaboration with The National Child Traumatic Stress Network (NCTSN) and its long-standing focus on trauma-informed screening and assessment. In particular, we offer our appreciation for the NCTSN Trauma and Screening Assessment Subcommittee and the NCTSN Complex Trauma & Developmental Trauma Disorders Workgroup, as much of their collective insight and knowledge was integrated into this work.

We would also like to offer our gratitude to the work of the Center for Child Trauma Assessment, Services and Interventions at Northwestern University Feinberg School of Medicine, given their ongoing emphasis on comprehensive assessment strategies and the meaningful application of trauma-informed assessments in practice, as well as their focus on elucidating the concept of assessment translation, which is critical to this book. We would also like to thank the Chadwick Center for Children and Families at Rady Children's Hospital–San Diego, which has done extensive work in the area of trauma assessment for the Trauma Assessment Pathway Model. Much of the work of these two organizations has informed the content of this book.

Trauma-Informed
Assessment With
Children and Adolescents

1 INTRODUCTION

Understanding the Rationale for and Benefits of Trauma-Informed Assessment

Angela[1] was 12 years old when she came in for treatment in a children's hospital. She was referred for treatment because of complaints of "bizarre behavior" in different settings; these behaviors included frequently placing a trash can on her head, avoiding eye contact with others, being unable to relate to her peers, and showing signs of auditory and visual hallucinations. By the time she was referred to the mental health clinic for therapy, she had received an initial evaluation and was given a diagnosis of psychotic disorder not otherwise specified. She was placed on Haldol (haloperidol), an antipsychotic drug, to treat her atypical and psychoticlike symptoms. However, in initial meetings with Angela in the mental health setting, the therapist observed that this diagnosis did not seem to fit.

After a more careful and trauma-informed assessment was conducted with Angela and other members of her family, the root of these difficulties appeared to be related not to psychosis, but rather to the ongoing and active domestic violence, physical abuse, and substance abuse that were taking place within her home. These traumatic and adverse experiences were not inquired about during her initial evaluation. Furthermore, what had previously appeared to be hallucinations, including Angela's symptoms of seeing and

---

[1] The case examples used throughout this book are fictitious or represent composites of actual cases; the confidentiality of real clients has been maintained.

https://doi.org/10.1037/0000233-001
Trauma-Informed Assessment With Children and Adolescents: Strategies to Support Clinicians, by C. Kisiel, T. Fehrenbach, L. Conradi, and L. Weil

hearing things that were not real, were actually manifestations of severe flashbacks in relation to her traumatic experiences.

In the process of receiving mental health services, a safety plan was established for Angela and her family. Angela's diagnosis and treatment plan were adjusted to address the trauma-related nature of her difficulties.

The prevalence of exposure to trauma among children and adolescents is increasingly recognized both in the general population and across child-serving settings (e.g., mental health, child welfare, juvenile justice, medical settings; Abram et al., 2004; Darnell et al., 2019; Greeson et al., 2011; Ko et al., 2008). Yet trauma exposure and its impact may not be accurately identified, and therefore referrals for mental health or trauma-informed assessment may not occur, even when appropriate or indicated on the basis of the needs of youth. As a result, responses to trauma may not be understood and subsequently may be mislabeled or misdiagnosed. This lack of understanding poses several challenges and can have detrimental consequences for the child and family over time and over the course of services.

Clinicians and other providers working in mental health settings are likely to work with youth who have experienced trauma, and many have likely faced challenges around potential mislabeling, misdiagnosis, or misunderstanding of the broad impact of trauma. In this book, we highlight the importance and benefits of trauma-informed assessment in addressing these issues and offer strategies for conducting comprehensive and effective trauma-informed assessments that can be used in practice to support the treatment planning and intervention process, engagement and education with families, and collaboration and advocacy with other providers and systems.

According to the National Child Traumatic Stress Network (NCTSN; n.d.), a *traumatic event* in childhood is "a frightening, dangerous, or violent event that poses a threat to a child's life or bodily integrity. Witnessing a traumatic event that threatens life or physical security of a loved one can also be traumatic" (para. 1). An estimated 2 million to 3 million children are victims of maltreatment (i.e., child abuse or neglect) each year (Children's Bureau, 2018), and nationwide community studies indicate that between 25% and 61% of children and adolescents are exposed to at least one traumatic event (Briggs et al., 2013; Gerson & Rappaport, 2013).

The term *adverse childhood experience* (ACE) is also often used to describe a traumatic or adverse experience in a person's life that occurs before age 18, consistent with the widely recognized ACE Study (see Chapter 3, this volume, for more on this study; Felitti et al., 1998; Sacks et al., 2014; U.S. Census Bureau, 2018). Moreover, data from the Health Resources and Services Administration's 2016 National Survey of Children's Health indicate that 46% of U.S. youth (including 34 million children under age 18) experienced at least one ACE and that 20% experienced at least two ACEs (U.S. Census Bureau, 2018).

Statistics on trauma exposure across child-serving settings suggest that between 34% and 44% of school-age children were exposed to at least one trauma in their family or community setting (Blodgett & Lanigan, 2018; Gonzalez et al., 2016). Within mental health settings, estimates of trauma exposure are up to 83% for youth presenting for outpatient services (Darnell et al., 2019) and up to 96% for adolescent psychiatric inpatients (Stein et al., 2001). For youth served in child welfare and juvenile justice settings, rates of exposure to at least one traumatic event are as high as 90% (Abram et al., 2004; Greeson et al., 2011; Stein et al., 2001), with at least half of these youth reporting exposure to multiple traumatic events (Abram et al., 2004; Finkelhor et al., 2011; Greeson et al., 2011; Stein et al., 2001).

Furthermore, among youth in child-serving settings, exposure to chronic trauma (i.e., repeated trauma) or complex trauma (i.e., multiple interpersonal traumas on an ongoing or repeated basis) is also common, particularly among those in the child welfare and juvenile justice systems (Habib & Labruna, 2011). However, despite the prevalence of trauma exposure, trauma-related issues are not always clearly identified or assessed; indeed, sometimes these issues are overlooked in mental health and other child-serving settings (Fallot & Harris, 2001), as illustrated in the case example of Angela.

High rates of trauma exposure among children and adolescents across settings speak to the paramount importance of offering what has been termed "trauma-informed care" (Darnell et al., 2019). *Trauma-informed care* refers to a

> strengths-based framework that is grounded in an understanding of and responsiveness to the impact of trauma, that emphasizes physical, psychological, and emotional safety for both providers and survivors, and that creates opportunities for survivors to rebuild a sense of control and empowerment. (Hopper et al., 2010, p. 82)

Over the past decade, the field of child trauma has made significant progress in defining, measuring, and promoting the concept of trauma-informed care both at the individual and family level and at the organizational level. Some authors have specifically discussed the need for integrating a trauma lens when working within child-serving systems (e.g., mental health, child welfare, juvenile justice) in which the majority of youth have been exposed to traumatic events (Ko et al., 2008; Taylor & Siegfried, 2005). The principles of trauma-informed care are described in Chapter 2.

Identifying and assessing the range of needs of children and adolescents exposed to trauma is an important first step in providing trauma-informed care and addressing these needs in the context of interventions. As clinicians and other providers strive to offer the best possible care to youth served in mental health and other settings, screening and assessment are a critical part of this process. However, confusion remains around what constitutes trauma-informed assessment, how this differs from trauma-informed screening, and who is responsible or most appropriate for conducting each of these processes.

The terms "screening" and "assessment" are often used interchangeably, but in practice they are intended to achieve different purposes; they are conducted at different points in the service delivery process, often by different providers. *Trauma screening* is a brief inquiry into whether a child or other individual has been exposed to or impacted by trauma. Screening typically involves a brief tool that is completed by frontline or direct service staff in service settings including child welfare, juvenile justice, school, and mental health or behavioral health. Trauma screening is generally used to identify exposure to traumatic events but also can include items specific to traumatic stress symptoms or reactions; this information is used to determine whether a child (or other individual) needs to be referred for a trauma-informed assessment or needs trauma-informed services (Conradi et al., 2011; Fallot & Harris, 2001; Kisiel, Conradi, et al., 2014).

Given the potential for underrecognition of trauma, many service systems have adopted a universal screening approach, asking all children and families receiving services about their trauma experiences, often as a part of the initial intake process. This screening is often done as part of an effort to become trauma informed and to raise awareness about trauma (Fallot & Harris, 2001). When universal screening is appropriate to incorporate, not only does this process more accurately and effectively screen for trauma, but it also communicates to the individuals and families being served that understanding the impact of trauma is a priority and that agency staff are willing and able to discuss trauma-related issues in the context of services (Fallot & Harris, 2001). It is important to note that trauma screening is designed as a brief inquiry and is not intended for diagnostic purposes (Kisiel, Conradi, et al., 2014).

Trauma-informed assessment is a comprehensive process designed to provide a detailed understanding of a child's trauma history, how trauma has impacted the child's functioning, including trauma-related symptoms or needs, and the severity of the child's experiences and symptoms (Conradi et al., 2011; Fallot & Harris, 2001). Trauma-informed assessments are typically conducted by trained mental health providers or clinicians, given the range of clinical issues to be explored and the need for in-depth exploration into the impact of trauma on a range of areas of functioning; therefore, facilitating this process often requires greater clinical understanding and training. The assessment process is often used to determine how trauma has impacted the child's development and acquisition of key skills and to determine goals and priorities for treatment based on the needs identified. The information gathered in a trauma-informed assessment can contribute to or result in diagnostic decisions for the child, as well (Fallot & Harris, 2001; Kisiel, Conradi, et al., 2014).

A comprehensive trauma-informed assessment process is a structured approach for gathering information and identifying and addressing the range of needs of children and families who have experienced trauma (including trauma-related symptoms, risk behaviors, and functional difficulties), as well as the strengths of the child, caregivers, and family. All of this information is used, ideally, to guide and support the treatment planning process (Conradi et al., 2011; Kisiel, Conradi, et al., 2014; Kisiel, Torgersen, et al., 2018).

Given the clinical relevance and importance of trauma-informed assessment, it typically occurs at the outset of mental health treatment in order to identify the primary presenting problems and help determine the goals and priorities for treatment. Furthermore, given its comprehensive nature and the range of recommended techniques (described throughout this book), a trauma-informed assessment often takes place over the course of several sessions (e.g., two to three sessions or more; Conradi et al., 2011; Kisiel, Conradi, et al., 2014). This multisession process not only allows for gathering an array of important information from the child and family but also offers the opportunity for the clinician and family to discuss their understanding of areas of need and the challenges these needs may pose for the child and family. In addition, this process creates the opportunity for identifying the areas that are going well for the child and emerging strengths that may support the child and family in the midst of these challenges. As a result, trauma-informed assessment can offer an important avenue for the early stages of child and family engagement in the treatment process (Fallot & Harris, 2001; Kisiel, Conradi, et al., 2014).

In addition to taking into consideration the guidelines and parameters within a given agency or setting, it is recommended that an initial assessment process take place, as well as an ongoing or reassessment process (e.g., after

3 or 6 months or at some other point). The reassessment process can be a more condensed version of the initial assessment and is useful in determining whether progress has been made toward the identified treatment goals (e.g., reduction in symptoms, increase in positive outcomes or strengths) or whether adjustments need to be made to the treatment plan or process. This reassessment process is discussed in more detail in Chapter 2.

An essential part of an effective trauma-informed assessment is consolidating and summarizing the information gathered from a range of sources and perspectives so that it can be translated and communicated to others (e.g., family members, other providers) and integrated into the treatment plan (Kisiel, Conradi, et al., 2014). This approach provides a pathway to effective treatment planning and the delivery of appropriate services that are responsive to the diverse needs of families and also incorporate their strengths and resources. It is important to note, however, that many clinicians are trained to view the assessment process as different or separate from the treatment process, rather than as an integral part of the beginning stages of treatment. Although we recognize that in many settings the same clinician or therapist is responsible for conducting both the assessment and treatment, in other settings the assessor is a different individual from the treating clinician. For instance, a trainee may be responsible for assessment or treatment, or a clinic may designate a specific staff person to conduct assessments (e.g., an intake assessor) and make referrals for the most appropriate type of treatment on the basis of the results. In any scenario, it is important that direct coordination and communication take place between assessor and mental health clinician in order to facilitate the most effective engagement and treatment process. Throughout this book, we encourage providers to consider assessment a key part of the intervention process, beginning with the initial engagement of children and families and continuing as assessment feedback is offered to guide, inform, and adjust the focus of treatment as needed.

FRAMEWORK FOR A TRAUMA-INFORMED ASSESSMENT

Over the past several years, advances have been made in defining and summarizing a framework for guiding an effective trauma-informed assessment approach (see Kisiel, Conradi, et al., 2014; Kisiel, Torgersen, et al., 2018; Strand et al., 2005). In brief, this framework is designed to support the successful implementation of a trauma-informed assessment process by providing

- a series of essential process elements, to be embedded within the organization, that are foundational in nature and designed to equip clinicians and the organization to implement a trauma-informed assessment process that is sustainable over time;

- a comprehensive process, including assessment across various domains and incorporation of multiple techniques and measures or tools and a range of perspectives and reporters;

- an organizing structure for gathering and making sense of information about needs and strengths of the child, caregiver, and family;

- a mechanism for summarizing and integrating assessment information for use in practice;

- input that informs and guides both the assessment and treatment or service planning in a developmentally sensitive and culturally responsive way;

- support for the selection of appropriate assessment tools and intervention approaches and monitoring of the outcomes of services;

- a process that facilitates engagement, the sharing of assessment feedback, and education for children and families during assessment and treatment; and

- a means to support communication, collaboration, and advocacy for trauma-informed services with other providers and across systems.

The overarching focus of this book is to highlight and explore in detail this framework for a comprehensive trauma-informed assessment approach and to offer strategies and examples to help clinicians put this approach into practice in their settings.

CONTEXT FOR TRAUMA-INFORMED ASSESSMENT: KEY ISSUES AND CHALLENGES

Although many strides have been made in outlining the components of an effective or "ideal" trauma-informed assessment process, there still exist several challenges in incorporating these components in practice.

The process of trauma-informed assessment for children and adolescents can still be improved and enhanced across settings. As described above, despite the prevalence of trauma exposure among youth across service settings, trauma-related issues may still be overlooked, mislabeled, or unassessed by providers within clinical settings (Kisiel, Fehrenbach, et al., 2014; van der Kolk, 2005). Many public child-serving settings still lack systematic and comprehensive trauma-informed assessment protocols, and providers may receive minimal or no information about a youth's trauma history during the referral process, despite the evidence that many youth in these systems have experienced significant trauma (Hanson et al., 2002; Kisiel, Fehrenbach, et al., 2014; Ko et al., 2008; Mahoney et al., 2004; Taylor & Siegfried, 2005). Certain factors may contribute to this oversight, including the underreporting of trauma by youth or caregivers and the underrecognition of trauma by providers, who may not fully understand or appreciate the importance of incorporating a trauma-informed approach in their work (Fallot & Harris, 2001; Kisiel, Conradi, et al., 2014). In addition, assessment protocols that are in place within clinical settings may include general mental health assessments, with tools assessing mental health symptoms or diagnoses, but often do not include trauma history or exposure questions or tools. These areas are explored further in subsequent chapters as they relate to the issue of differential diagnosis and possible misdiagnosis among youth with trauma histories (Fallot & Harris, 2001).

There are several reasons why trauma-informed screening or assessment processes may not be incorporated as a standard part of practice. One reason may be related to potential difficulties with recognizing and identifying the range of trauma experiences and trauma-related issues among youth within a particular setting, as described above. Another reason is the additional resource challenges that may arise when youth are identified as having trauma-related needs and require referral to trauma-focused intervention services, which may not be readily available (Fallot & Harris, 2001; Kisiel, Conradi, et al., 2014; Kisiel, Patterson, et al., 2018). In addition, there may be challenges with the time and resources associated with conducting a trauma-informed assessment. As described previously, conducting an initial comprehensive assessment over the course of a few sessions and then a follow-up assessment can be time consuming. When there are staff or resource constraints within a given setting (e.g., limited staff capacity to conduct a comprehensive assessment, financial constraints on purchasing tools when required), there may be a tendency to gather a narrower range of information over a shorter period of time.

Furthermore, providers may lack education on child trauma or training on how to effectively incorporate trauma assessment information into practice with children and families or in the context of treatment planning. This lack of provider education and training may contribute to the tendency to avoid the use of trauma-informed assessment tools (Fallot & Harris, 2001; Kisiel, Patterson, et al., 2018); additional resources and training are needed to support the meaningful application of trauma-informed assessment in practice (Kisiel, Fehrenbach, et al., 2014; Kisiel, Torgersen, et al., 2018). Providers' discomfort or uncertainty around what to do with trauma-related information once collected or how to address trauma with children and families may also contribute to the omission of assessment for trauma exposure and its impact on children and families. For instance, providers may avoid asking about trauma-related needs in the context of an assessment when there are no corresponding services or interventions available in the geographic area (Fallot & Harris, 2001).

An additional challenge to incorporating trauma-informed screening or assessment as a standard part of practice may arise when clinicians try to explain the findings to children and families or translate findings in the context of treatment planning or intervention. This challenge may be related to the fact that several existing trauma-informed assessment tools were designed primarily for research purposes without an emphasis on direct application or clinical utility (Kisiel, Patterson, et al., 2018; Lyons, 2009). There is a need for more consistent staff training and educational resources to support application of trauma assessment in clinical practice (Kisiel, Conradi, et al., 2014; Kisiel, Patterson, et al., 2018). These issues are highlighted in subsequent chapters, and practical applications and tips are embedded throughout this book.

Finally, when describing the recommended or "ideal" trauma-informed assessment process throughout this book, we recognize that the process does not always happen fully in practice and that there may be constraints or challenges with embedding this approach to its fullest extent within practice settings. Therefore, throughout the book we highlight the challenges associated with implementing recommendations in mental health practice settings and provide practical strategies or solutions for addressing these issues when challenges occur. Furthermore, it is important to note that several of the guidelines and suggestions provided in relation to the process and meaningful application of trauma-informed assessment build on literature that initially outlined this framework and related concepts (see Kisiel, Conradi, et al., 2014; Kisiel, Torgersen, et al., 2018) without accompanying empirical support. These recommendations are based on practical wisdom, clinical insights, and feedback from youth and caregivers across various settings as well as the collective experiences of the authors and their colleagues in their work in trauma-focused mental health centers. More research is needed to fully understand the impact of applying these processes broadly across a range of service settings.

Assessment is one of the critical first steps in understanding and addressing the complex needs of youth impacted by trauma; it is important for conceptualizing and prioritizing treatment goals, recommendations, and interventions for youth served in various settings (Kisiel, Blaustein, et al., 2009). However, it is important to note that even when a comprehensive trauma-informed assessment is conducted, children served in mental health settings and other systems (e.g., child welfare, juvenile justice) may still fall through the cracks. They may receive a range of diagnoses or unnecessary medication, and they may never receive appropriate trauma-informed care from the very systems that are supposed to help them recover, heal, and rehabilitate (Kisiel, Fehrenbach, et al., 2014; Kisiel, Torgersen, et al., 2018).

Although some mental health agencies identify themselves as providing more "general" mental health services for children compared with other agencies that focus specifically on trauma-informed services, we argue that all mental health agencies would benefit from implementing a trauma-informed assessment approach (at least to some degree), given the high prevalence of trauma among youth served across settings. Therefore, it is paramount that all mental health professionals work to improve their trauma-informed assessment processes, to more clearly link assessment with appropriate and effective trauma-informed services for youth and families, to increase trauma training and education for providers, and to enhance communication, information sharing, and advocacy across service systems and with families. This work will help support a greater understanding of trauma-related needs and greater transparency in the trauma-informed services required for these youth.

DESCRIPTION AND ORGANIZATION OF THIS BOOK

Although several books have addressed the topic of child trauma assessment, no resource is available that integrates recommendations for trauma-informed assessment approaches for children and adolescents, including domains to assess and tools to consider, with clinical applications for the meaningful use of these tools and approaches in practice. This book draws on and summarizes the existing clinical, theoretical, and empirical literature, which serves as a basis for most of the practical strategies provided in each chapter. It is our intention that this book provide an efficient and effective opportunity for clinicians (both in practice and in training) and other professionals to become familiar with the current trauma assessment literature and simultaneously to benefit from real-world examples and recommendations in a way that will help them apply this knowledge in a meaningful way.

This book is unique in that it offers an overview of and rationale for a comprehensive approach to trauma-informed assessment with children and adolescents, including key domains and techniques. It also suggests a range of recommended tools and considerations for selecting and using the tools across stages of development and in relation to sociocultural context. The book also explores the process elements and meaningful applications of trauma-informed assessment in clinical practice with children and families and in collaboration with other providers and service systems, and it offers practical strategies and techniques for doing so.

Addressing Gaps in Trauma-Informed Assessment: Content Overview

Although much progress has been made in the area of trauma-informed assessment, there are still relative and important gaps in the literature regarding how to provide the highest quality care to youth and families impacted by trauma. One such gap in the current literature is how to conduct a trauma-informed assessment in an organized, structured, comprehensive, culturally attuned, meaningful, and collaborative way, with youth and families as partners in the process. This book addresses this gap by providing a resource to enhance provider knowledge, promote staff training and education, and guide clinicians on how to conduct a comprehensive trauma-informed assessment in the context of clinical practice and integrate trauma-informed assessment in the context of engaging families and as part of the clinical intervention process.

Throughout the book we emphasize how the evidence for the use of assessment tools and techniques translates into best practices when assessing trauma-exposed children and adolescents from diverse backgrounds. We also review challenges that may arise in the context of a trauma-informed assessment (based on the topic areas noted above) and suggest strategies to overcome these barriers. This book does not, however, provide an in-depth exploration of all the possible domains for assessment and the supporting literature across these domains; rather, it provides a brief overview of these areas with supporting evidence and questions to guide the assessment process. It also offers practitioner-friendly guidance for clinicians and other professionals working with children and adolescents exposed to trauma. Whereas this book offers suggestions for relevant tools related to child trauma, it is not intended to provide an exhaustive review of or specific recommendations for available tools; these areas are addressed more fully in other recent books and articles (see Nader, 2008b, 2014).

Content Organization

The contents of this book are organized according to the following topic areas:

- Chapter 1 highlighted the rationale for and benefits of a comprehensive trauma-informed assessment approach.

- Chapter 2 describes the key principles and essential organizational process elements to consider in implementing trauma-informed assessment, including providing clinician training, establishing a safe environment, engaging families, integrating standardized tools, using clinical supervision, and viewing assessment as an ongoing process.

- Chapter 3 discusses the implementation of a comprehensive trauma-informed assessment, providing an overview and detailing the key domains of trauma-informed assessment and the recommended structure and techniques for gathering information. The key domains include the various areas to assess related to child, family, and caregiver history, responses, and functioning. The structure offers an overview of the range of assessment techniques and approaches to consider, including the importance of incorporating multiple informants or perspectives, with suggestions for consolidating and integrating this information for use in practice.

- Chapter 4 describes issues for consideration in tailoring the trauma-informed assessment to the individual youth and their development and sociocultural context.

- Chapter 5 offers considerations for selecting and integrating trauma-informed assessment tools and provides a review of recommended assessment tools to assess various domains.

- Chapter 6 describes collaborative and meaningful applications of trauma-informed assessment in practice, including techniques for the translation of assessment information to clinical practice.

- Chapter 7 summarizes key recommendations and discusses potential future directions for research and trauma-informed assessment practice.

Use of Terminology

A brief note is in order about the use of specific terms and language in this book. The terms used to describe the providers involved in the assessment process—for instance, "clinician," "mental health provider," and "therapist"— are used interchangeably to describe the primary individuals conducting a trauma-informed assessment. These individuals may be master's- or doctoral-level clinicians with various types of training and education. The terms "providers" and "professionals" are used more broadly to refer to the range of staff providing services to children and families across various systems.

The terms "children" and "adolescents" are used to refer to young people at these two developmental stages; the terms "children" and "youth" are used interchangeably to refer to both young children and adolescents. When referring to parents and caregivers, the term "caregivers" is inclusive of both biological parents and other adult caregivers, including foster parents. Finally, the terms "clients" and "patients" are used to refer to the children and families receiving mental health services as these terms are commonly used in clinical settings.

The term "tool" refers to any assessment tool, instrument, or measure, unless a different term is specified in the name or by the developer. The terms "key" and "essential" are used to describe the primary or integral areas for consideration or steps to guide the various facets of assessment (e.g., in relation to assessment domains used to gather information or processes for gathering this information in a trauma-informed manner). The term "trauma-informed assessment" is used to describe the main focus of this book, a process conducted by trained clinicians often occurring prior to or in conjunction with mental health treatment. At times, the phrase "comprehensive trauma-informed assessment" is used to describe this same process, particularly when defining its components. In any case, trauma-informed assessment is meant to be comprehensive in nature, encompassing the range of domains, techniques, and perspectives recommended (described in Chapter 3).

It may be important to clarify that the trauma-informed assessment process is not intended to describe psychological evaluation or diagnostic testing. Psychological evaluation is a comprehensive, diagnostic evaluation of all domains of functioning in a child, including cognitive, developmental, social–emotional, and personality functioning; it is typically completed in response to a specific referral question (Conradi et al., 2011). Although the processes of screening, assessment, and psychological evaluation can exist along a continuum, and there may be some overlap in the specific tools used within these different processes, it is important to note that these are all distinct processes with different purposes. This distinction is addressed further in Chapter 4.

Intended Audiences

The primary audience for this book includes clinicians and therapists who conduct trauma-informed assessments or offer clinical services to children and adolescents. This audience also includes graduate students who are receiving clinical training and education in working with children and families, as the book offers an overview of basic concepts and approaches when conducting a trauma-informed assessment. A secondary audience includes other service providers who conduct trauma screenings that inform assessments and those who collaborate with clinicians who are conducting trauma-informed assessments. The practical recommendations included throughout this book can be applied across a range of child-serving systems. For instance, this material may be relevant to supervisors and administrators working in nonprofit agencies and state-level systems that provide services to traumatized youth and families. We believe this book holds the most potential for moving the field forward when it is regularly used within graduate training programs, internship settings, and staff training programs in which clinicians initially learn about and gain experiences with conducting assessments with children and families.

Clinicians may face unique challenges when conducting trauma-informed assessments that are comprehensive and meaningful while working within the time and resource constraints of mental health providers and agencies. This book is intended to offer an overview of trauma-informed assessment, areas for consideration and suggested tools and techniques for clinicians seeking to incorporate or improve their use of trauma-informed assessment, and strategies for effectively integrating trauma-informed assessment in meaningful ways in the context of clinical interventions or practices. Given its focus on summarizing current research and articulating practical and meaningful recommendations for providers on trauma-informed assessment, our hope is that this book will support and enhance the trauma-informed care provided to youth and families who have experienced trauma.

2

KEY PRINCIPLES AND ESSENTIAL ORGANIZATIONAL PROCESS ELEMENTS OF TRAUMA-INFORMED ASSESSMENT

For clinicians to effectively implement and integrate trauma-informed assessment in their practice, it is important to consider the broader agency or organizational framework within which they are conducting assessments. Several essential organizational process elements need to be considered to support comprehensive trauma-informed assessment for children and adolescents. These essential process elements are foundational in nature and are designed to equip the clinician and organization to implement trauma-informed assessment sustainably over time. For instance, it is not uncommon for clinicians to become frustrated when they are expected to conduct trauma-informed assessments if they do not receive the larger organizational support to do so effectively. Therefore, considering how these elements apply specifically to the settings in which clinicians are conducting assessments is critical.

This chapter begins by outlining six key principles of a trauma-informed approach as identified by the Substance Abuse and Mental Health Services Administration (SAMHSA; 2014). It then discusses the six essential organizational process elements of a trauma-informed assessment framework.

https://doi.org/10.1037/0000233-002
Trauma-Informed Assessment With Children and Adolescents: Strategies to Support Clinicians, by C. Kisiel, T. Fehrenbach, L. Conradi, and L. Weil

Organizational leaders and agency staff are encouraged to consider these essential process elements in order to support the successful implementation of trauma-informed assessment. The six essential organizational process elements are

1. training clinicians on conducting a trauma-informed assessment,
2. creating a safe environment at the agency or organization and within the assessment itself,
3. engaging the child and family as active participants,
4. integrating evidence-based tools and processes,
5. using clinical supervision to support the trauma-informed assessment, and
6. viewing trauma-informed assessment as an ongoing practice.

Concrete suggestions for ways to effectively integrate each component are provided. Challenges and practical considerations for both clinicians and organizations are also addressed.

KEY PRINCIPLES OF A TRAUMA-INFORMED APPROACH

The effective implementation of a trauma-informed assessment process must occur within a broader trauma-informed approach. According to SAMHSA (2014), there are four *R*s of a trauma-informed approach within a program, organization, or system:

1. *Realize* the widespread impact of trauma and understand potential paths for recovery;
2. *Recognize* the signs and symptoms of trauma in clients, families, staff, and others involved with the system;
3. *Respond* by fully integrating knowledge about trauma into policies, procedures, and practices; and
4. Seek to actively *Resist* retraumatization (SAMHSA, 2014, pp. 9–10).

Trauma-informed assessment provides a mechanism by which the clinician can gather information on a youth's trauma history and responses in a thoughtful and organized way. This information is then integrated into the broader understanding of the youth within the context of those experiences and informs treatment and service planning efforts.

SAMHSA (2014, pp. 10–11) described a trauma-informed approach at the agency level that includes six key principles designed to provide a broad framework to integrate trauma-informed practices and to support a flexible, rather than rigid, set of practices and procedures:

1. *Safety*—Throughout the organization, staff members and the individuals they serve feel physically and psychologically safe, and all interactions promote a sense of safety.

2. *Trustworthiness and transparency*—Organizational operations and decisions are conducted with transparency and with the goal of building and maintaining trust among staff, clients, and family members. Establishing trustworthiness and transparency includes maximizing trust, making tasks clear, and maintaining appropriate boundaries with clients.

3. *Peer support*—Peer support is integral to the organizational and service delivery approach and is understood as a key vehicle for building trust, establishing safety, and promoting empowerment. Peer support includes a process in which individuals support one another through the use of stories and lived experience to promote recovery and healing.

4. *Collaboration and mutuality*—There is true partnering and leveling of power differences between staff and the children and youth served, as well as among organizational staff from direct care staff to administrators. The organization recognizes that everyone has a role to play in a trauma-informed approach; a person does not have to be a therapist to be therapeutic. There is recognition that healing happens in relationships and in the meaningful sharing of power and decision making.

5. *Empowerment, voice, and choice*—Throughout the organization and among the clients served, individuals' strengths are recognized, built on, and validated and new skills developed as necessary. The organization aims to strengthen the staff's, clients', and family members' experience of choice and recognizes that every person's experience is unique and requires an individualized approach. This principle includes a belief in resilience and in the ability of individuals, organizations, and communities to heal and promote recovery from trauma. This approach builds on what clients, staff, and communities have to offer, rather than responding to perceived deficits.

6. *Cultural, historical, and gender issues*—The organization actively moves past cultural stereotypes and biases (based on, e.g., race, ethnicity, sexual orientation, age, geography), offers gender-responsive services, leverages the healing value of traditional cultural connections, and recognizes and addresses historical and racial trauma. The organization demonstrates knowledge of how specific social and cultural groups may experience, react to, and recover from trauma differently while being proactive in respectfully seeking information and learning about differences among

social and cultural groups. The organization can easily access support and resources for sensitively meeting the unique social and cultural needs of others.

Whereas SAMHSA's (2014) six key principles of a trauma-informed approach are intended to be understood from a wider agency or systems perspective, they also provide a helpful lens through which to view the process of trauma-informed assessment more broadly. Later sections in this chapter provide more specific information as to how these trauma-informed principles can be applied within the context of a trauma-informed assessment.

ESSENTIAL ORGANIZATIONAL PROCESS ELEMENTS OF TRAUMA-INFORMED ASSESSMENT

Before implementing trauma-informed assessment, organizational leaders and agency staff are encouraged to consider the six essential organizational process elements designed to create and support the assessment infrastructure and to apply SAMHSA's (2014) trauma-informed principles.

Training Clinicians on Conducting a Trauma-Informed Assessment

The first essential organizational process element to consider when implementing a trauma-informed assessment process with children and adolescents is the training necessary to support clinicians in doing this work. The American Psychological Association (APA; 2015b) developed a list of trauma competencies that are aspirational in nature. It is recommended that organizations strive to put these competencies in place organizationally to support trauma-informed practice within the field of psychology. These competencies highlight both education and training, are designed to serve as a foundation for this work, and apply equally to clinicians conducting the assessment and those providing treatment. These guidelines include cross-cutting competencies as well as scientific knowledge, psychological assessment, psychological intervention, professionalism, and relational and systems competencies. Appendix A provides a description of and link to these guidelines.

Overall, clinicians ideally demonstrate a general understanding of the prevalence of child trauma and the impact of trauma on different developmental domains and areas of functioning. This competency may also include knowledge about identified protective and risk factors for child trauma, the range of symptom patterns, and the process of recovery over time. Further, having some understanding of how these patterns may differ by sub-population (e.g., gender, developmental level, trauma exposure pattern) and setting (e.g., mental health, juvenile justice, primary care) is also suggested.

In addition to training on knowledge competencies, organizational leaders are encouraged to provide clinicians with training on the trauma-informed assessment process itself. This element of training may include online or in-person training on the tools and the assessment process and ongoing consultation or supervision to support implementation and application efforts, such as integrating the findings from the assessment into treatment planning efforts and engaging the family in the assessment process (Kisiel, Torgersen, et al., 2018). Training ideally includes interactive and role-play elements that support the transfer of knowledge so that clinicians feel comfortable conducting these assessments.

Creating a Safe Environment

The second essential organizational process element of trauma-informed assessment is creating a safe environment for both the client and the clinician. For so long, the concept of safety has primarily focused on the provision of physical safety. Although ensuring physical safety is critically important (examples of strategies are provided in Exhibit 2.1), it is not the only type of safety that exists within a trauma-informed approach. One of the key impacts of trauma is that an individual may not *feel* safe in the world as a result of their experiences. Children and adolescents who have experienced trauma may have valid fears about their own safety or the safety of loved ones, and they may be hyperaware of potential threats in any new environment. As a result, they may respond by being hypervigilant to their surroundings, constantly looking for signs of threat. When faced with people, situations, places, or things that remind them of traumatic events, youth may reexperience intense and disturbing feelings tied to the original trauma. When a circumstance or event reminds them about their trauma, they may be triggered and respond to the new event in the same way they did to the original trauma, even if there is no actual threat.

In this sense, the child or adolescent may be physically safe, but they may not be emotionally safe, feeling that the world is not a safe place for them. *Emotional safety* is the sense of feeling safe with other people, in one's community, and within one's self (Bloom & Farragher, 2014). Individuals who have experienced traumatic events may go through the world feeling as though there is impending risk and threat around every corner, including

EXHIBIT 2.1. Strategies to Create a Physically and Emotionally Safe Environment During the Trauma-Informed Assessment Process

Strategies to Promote Physical Safety

- Confirm that the agency building is well lit, easy to find, accessible, clean, and comfortable.
- Ensure that the location and assessment process are protected from potential abusers, including caregivers who are the alleged perpetrator.
- Ensure that the directions to the agency's location are clear and readily available.
- Create a welcoming environment in the agency that includes directional signs and visual materials that demonstrate inclusivity and support.
- Ensure that the office where the assessment will be conducted is private and welcoming.
- Ensure that the client has adequate personal space and privacy to share information during the assessment process.
- Confirm that policies and procedures are in place to manage any crises that emerge, including disclosures of abuse and harm to self or others.
- Speak in a soft to normal volume, using a normal to low pitch and a slow, even tempo.

Strategies to Promote Emotional Safety

- Create stability and minimize unnecessary changes, and when changes are necessary, provide sufficient notice and preparation.
- Maintain healthy interpersonal boundaries and manage conflict appropriately in relationships with others.
- Use words to reflect the youth's experience.
- Ask open-ended but clear questions that allow the individual to share to their level of comfort.
- Be at the same level physically so the child feels more comfortable.
- Demonstrate interest in the child or adolescent through eye contact (if appropriate).
- Create opportunities for the family to experience a sense of control during the assessment process, such as by being given choices.
- Have an open, relaxed body posture.
- Have a positive facial expression.
- Listen and respond in a timely manner.
- Provide tools to manage emotional and physical reactions to sharing, such as deep breathing, meditation, and other techniques.
- When trauma is disclosed, recognize the seriousness of what the child or adolescent went through and empathize with their feelings.
- Try not to make assumptions about the impact of specific events, understanding that the impact of trauma is subjective in nature.
- Ask the child or adolescent whether there are areas or topics that are off limits because of their culture or personal preferences.
- Invite the child or adolescent and family to ask questions throughout the process.
- Provide a clear rationale for asking about difficult or personal topics.
- Remind the child and family that they are in charge of how much they want to share and how much detail they are comfortable sharing, acknowledging that it may be difficult to open up to someone they don't know well.

during the trauma-informed assessment process. When a client comes in for a trauma-informed assessment, it may be the first time they come into the agency and meet the clinician. During this meeting, the clinician asks them questions about their history, requesting information about their trauma experiences, which they may have never disclosed before. As a result, a trauma-informed assessment can be an extremely novel and vulnerability-provoking experience, in which the social conventions of what is typically shared with a stranger are turned upside down. Therefore, it is critical to ensure that the youth experiences the interaction with the clinician as both physically and emotionally safe. Exhibit 2.1 lists strategies to help clinicians create an emotionally safe environment during the assessment process (Harris & Fallot, 2001). Additional strategies for promoting physical and emotional safety are discussed in Chapter 4.

An important component in increasing a child's or adolescent's sense of safety during the assessment process is the clinician's awareness of their own anxiety about the process of asking questions about the youth's experience of trauma and subsequent symptoms. Sampson and Read (2017) found that clinicians in mental health clinics were not particularly good at asking about traumatic experiences or symptoms; the authors hypothesized that the clinicians felt uncomfortable in this process and would benefit from increased training on this issue.

This hypothesis receives some support from the literature focused on perceptions of distress when asking about abuse and trauma; numerous studies have explored clinicians' belief that participants will experience distress when asked questions regarding their victimization and trauma history. However, much of this research has found that participants do not experience such distress and, in fact, actually appreciate being asked the questions. For example, Black and colleagues (2006) found that 92% of participants felt that questions about trauma experience and symptoms should be asked. Moreover, Finkelhor et al. (2014) examined youths' experiences of answering questions about exposure to violence, sexual assault, and family maltreatment during the National Survey of Children Exposed to Violence. They found that only 4.5% reported being at all upset and that only 0.8% reported being pretty upset or a lot upset. Only a minority of those upset, 0.3% of the total sample, said they would not have participated had they known about the content of the interview.

Unfortunately, the research findings in this area are not all positive. In a telephone survey study examining the impact of asking sensitive questions on topics such as abuse and violence with adolescents ages 10 to 14, Ybarra and colleagues (2009) found that approximately a quarter of participants reported feeling upset when asked questions about violence. These mixed results suggest that it is not only the types of questions being asked, but also the training and comfort level of the clinician in asking the questions, that are critical when creating a safe environment during the assessment process.

Although supporting the youth and family to feel safe and comfortable during the trauma-informed assessment process is critical, it is also important to ensure that the clinician feels safe and comfortable both during and after the assessment. The following are some potential strategies to support the well-being of the clinician during this process and mitigate some of the potential impacts of hearing stories regarding a child's or adolescent's experience of trauma:

- checking in with oneself regarding feelings of physical and emotional safety.

- knowing how to handle a physical or emotional emergency or crisis and identifying potential triggers in the environment or in the behaviors of the child or adolescent being assessed.

- practicing mindfulness and grounding techniques. A large body of research has emerged in the area of mindfulness about how these practices can facilitate the connection between the emotional regulation and cognitive processing centers of the brain (Guendelman et al., 2017). Connecting these two centers of the brain plays a key role in allowing clinicians to be both emotionally present and able to provide guidance and support as needed.

- examining any emotional responses one may have to the information that has been shared. Exposure to material regarding a client's experiences of abuse or trauma has been connected to symptoms of secondary traumatic stress in clinicians (Figley, 1995; Salston & Figley, 2003). It is recommended that clinicians consistently examine their own responses and potential secondary traumatic stress reactions that may emerge in this process, which may include
  - avoidance of specific situations or clients;
  - preoccupation with clients or their stories;
  - intrusive thoughts, nightmares, or flashbacks;
  - arousal symptoms;
  - thoughts of violence or revenge;
  - feelings of estrangement or isolation or of having no one to talk to;

- feelings of being trapped, "infected" by trauma, hopeless, inadequate, or depressed; or
- difficulty separating work from personal life.

• discussing distressing situations and cases with a supervisor or peer, within the bounds of confidentiality, who will listen without judgment and respond with support and assistance. Guidance for discussing these topics in supervision is provided later in this chapter.

• consistently engaging in self-care and other activities that one identifies as recharging on an ongoing basis. These activities may include exercise, travel, mindfulness or meditation, and other types of self-care.

Engaging the Child and Family as Active Participants

Another essential organizational process element of trauma-informed assessment is engagement of the child and family as active participants throughout the assessment. Research has focused on overcoming many of the barriers to successful completion of treatment and identifying strategies to enhance clinical engagement. McKay and colleagues designed intensive engagement interventions that have effectively increased rates of service utilization and mental health treatment completion (Gopalan et al., 2010; McKay & Bannon, 2004). Many of these interventions include strategies that can be integrated into both the assessment and the treatment process, including

• clarifying the need for child mental health treatment for both the caregiver and the youth;

• maximizing the caregiver's investment and sense of efficacy in relation to help seeking;

• identifying attitudes about previous experiences with mental health care that might discourage the caregiver from bringing their child in for services; and

• developing strategies to overcome concrete (e.g., transportation, scheduling, child care), contextual (e.g., community violence), and agency (e.g., wait list, parking) obstacles.

Effectively engaging youth and families in the trauma-informed assessment process begins during the family's first contact with the agency, when the assessment meeting is scheduled (Kisiel, Torgersen, et al., 2018). It is important to share as much information about the assessment process as possible during the first assessment meeting and then to continue this transparency throughout the process. This information sharing includes explaining what will occur during the assessment (e.g., completion of measures, anticipated number of sessions), describing other sources of information the clinician will use to understand the child's functioning, and specifying how the assessment information will be used. This first meeting provides an important opportunity for initial engagement by clarifying the purpose and benefits of the assessment process, including an explanation of how fully understanding the youth's needs and strengths will enable the clinician to best help the family. Suggestions also include providing a clear, nonthreatening rationale for the assessment and being mindful about the timing of the assessment (e.g., avoiding anniversaries of traumatic events if possible). Chapter 6 focuses on engaging families as collaborative partners in the trauma-informed assessment process.

Integrating Evidence-Based Tools and Processes

The integration of evidence-based tools and processes is another essential organizational process element of a trauma-informed assessment framework. This process element includes ensuring that the assessment is conducted in a structured manner that incorporates knowledge of best practices and research evidence for the tools and processes that are used. A couple of terms have been used to describe the concepts in this process element. For example, "evidence-based assessment" refers to the use of research and theory to inform the selection of constructs to assess, the methods and measures used in the assessment, and the assessment process itself (Hunsley & Mash, 2007). Another term, "measurement-based care" (MBC), refers not only to the framework of the assessment process itself but also to the practice of reassessing the efficacy of services using clinical data gathered through the assessment process (Scott & Lewis, 2015). In MBC, measurement tools are administered over time to assess changes in symptom presentation (use of measurement tools is discussed at length in Chapter 5). However, rather than merely incorporating tools, MBC highlights the importance of using the tools to provide insights into treatment progress, emphasize ongoing treatment targets, reduce symptom deterioration, and improve client outcomes (Lambert et al., 2005).

This essential process element can be particularly challenging as, historically, clinicians have been somewhat uncertain about incorporating tools into their assessment process, questioning whether the value added is comparable to their own clinical insights and experiences (J. R. Cook et al., 2017;

Meehl, 1996). To use this process effectively, clinicians are encouraged to select tools that have reliability (i.e., are consistent over time) and validity (i.e., measure what they are intended to measure) and that can be used to measure change over time. Clinicians are encouraged to undertake the assessment process itself with a degree of rigor, to formulate a picture of what they are hoping to accomplish during the assessment itself, and to incorporate tools and processes that have evidence to support their use in these settings. A discussion of available tools and the relative merits of each is provided in Chapter 5.

Using Clinical Supervision to Support the Trauma-Informed Assessment

Regardless of the amount of training or experience the clinician has, supervision is a critical component of work with cases involving child trauma. According to APA (2014), *supervision* is defined as

> a distinct professional practice employing a collaborative relationship that has both facilitative and evaluative components, that extends over time, which has the goals of enhancing the professional competence and science-informed practice of the supervisee, monitoring the quality of services provided, protecting the public, and providing a gatekeeping function for entry into the profession. (p. 2)

Just as the relationship between the client and clinician forms the glue that allows clinical work to take place, the relationship between the clinician and supervisor creates a safe environment in which the clinician can discuss the complexities and intricacies of these difficult cases, track treatment progress, and process countertransference issues (Tawfik et al., 2016). Although it is helpful for clinicians to have the support of a clinical supervisor throughout the assessment process, supervision may not be readily available for some agency-based, licensed clinicians because they officially no longer require supervision. This may also be the case for clinicians in private practice who work independently without existing supervisory structures in place. For these clinicians, it would be helpful to seek out peer supervision to provide the necessary supports for effectively managing the complexity of the trauma-informed assessment process. Peer supervision may include discussion of challenging cases with fellow clinicians within an organization who have relevant experience or participation in an external peer supervision group with other clinicians in the community while maintaining client confidentiality. In addition, when supervision or peer supervision occurs, there is increased certainty that the clinical work will remain on task as defined by treatment goals.

The process of supervision can also be used to ensure the accurate completion of a trauma-informed assessment by providing feedback or an additional perspective on the assessment administration and findings. This supervision may address the process used for the clinical interview, selection of appropriate measures, ways to make sense of the information collected, use of the information to direct treatment planning services, and monitoring of progress over time. Supervision may also be used to support the process of engaging family members in the assessment, sharing feedback, and engaging in collaborative treatment planning. Supervision may be done by coaching the clinician on effective strategies and addressing barriers to engagement and collaboration that may emerge (Kisiel, Torgersen, et al., 2018).

Supervision also plays a critical role in mitigating the impact of secondary traumatic stress on the clinician (A. Quinn et al., 2018). The Secondary Traumatic Stress Committee (2018) of the National Child Traumatic Stress Network developed a set of core competencies for supervisors in conducting trauma-informed supervision. Although the purview of these competencies is broader than assessment, they can be useful in supporting clinicians as they manage their reactions to hearing trauma-related information during the assessment process. These competencies address both knowledge, such as understanding the signs, symptoms, and risk factors of secondary traumatic stress, and practices, such as skills to assist clinicians in emotional reregulation after difficult encounters with clients. Appendix A provides a description of and link to these competencies. By supporting the clinician in developing these trauma-informed competencies, the supervisor also supports the clinician in monitoring their own responses during the assessment process, creating a safe environment to process potentially distressing information, and using the assessment process to link to trauma-informed service delivery efforts.

Viewing Trauma-Informed Assessment as an Ongoing Process

To ensure that each stage of treatment reflects the unique needs of the client, trauma-informed assessment must be an ongoing process that occurs throughout treatment, not just at the beginning. For example, the clinician may incorporate clinical interview questions and observations into each session with youth and caregivers. Further, many of the tools used during the clinical assessment process may be readministered because they are sensitive to change over time.

To track changes appropriately, it is important for a core set of tools to be readministered and completed at periodic intervals (e.g., every 3 months, every 6 months) by the same informants, if possible. Periodic readministration of standardized tools ensures that the client's progress is being monitored during treatment, noting new problems that emerge and strengths and resources that develop over time, as the clinician focuses on treatment tasks. Researchers recommend reassessing clients every 3 months, although that may be difficult logistically depending on other treatment demands, so it may be more reasonable to select longer assessment intervals. The reassessment process allows changes to be identified and incorporated into treatment plans and ensures that the clinician is selecting appropriate clinical interventions (Gothard et al., 2000). By continuing to gather assessment information, the clinician can respond to changing needs by updating the working clinical hypotheses, monitoring progress in treatment, and redirecting the course of treatment when indicated. Newly identified issues may strengthen the existing clinical hypotheses or lead to modified hypotheses.

Although symptom reduction is the ultimate goal of treatment, at times clinicians may note an increase in certain symptoms as identified in the results from assessment tools administered throughout treatment. For example, Gomes-Schwartz and colleagues (1990) found that about 18 months into treatment, sexually abused children showed an increase in fighting with both siblings and parents. Similarly, Lanktree and Briere (1995) found a marginally significant increase in anger at 1 year and a significant increase in sexual concerns after 9 months in sexual abuse treatment. Other researchers have found that these symptoms increase and then decline over the course of therapy (Berliner & Elliott, 2002). Finkelhor and Berliner (1995) referred to this pattern as a "reverse sleeper effect" and as "deterioration that is a sign of later improvement" (p. 1417). Clients who are not displaying clinical improvement on the assessment tools or who show an increase in symptoms may require a change in clinical hypotheses, treatment goals, or clinical interventions. It may also be helpful for the clinician to consider talking with the family about the therapeutic relationship and then address any concerns related to the relationship itself.

Regardless of whether the scores increase or decrease, the results from repeating some assessment measures over time provide concrete feedback to the clinician regarding the need to reevaluate the working hypotheses and goals. This iterative assessment process helps the clinician both determine the initial treatment plan and revise it as needed on an ongoing basis. Periodic reassessment also presents a good opportunity for clinicians to reevaluate whether a client would benefit from different treatment modalities, such as family or group therapy, and whether a psychiatric consultation or psychological testing is warranted.

CHALLENGES AND PRACTICAL CONSIDERATIONS FOR ORGANIZATIONS AND CLINICIANS

The essential organizational process elements of a trauma-informed assessment framework identified in this chapter reflect ideal assessment practices within a clinical setting. However, they have their own set of challenges and practical considerations. Establishing an effective trauma-informed assessment process takes time and resources and can involve ensuring that clinicians have access to training on trauma-informed assessment practices, that there is a safe and supportive environment to conduct assessments, that families are engaged at each step, and that ongoing supervision and support are provided. Further, the readministration of assessment tools over time requires that the organization invest time and resources in implementing a process in which clinicians know when to administer follow-up measures and how to score and apply their findings in a timely manner.

Therefore, it is critical that efforts be made at the individual and organizational level to create buy-in for these processes, while also providing tips and resources to support clinicians in their assessment practices. These efforts may include hiring personnel to manage the overall assessment process and to ensure that clinicians receive adequate training, monitor the completion of assessment measures, and identify when follow-up assessments should be completed. Another potential strategy is prioritizing these elements and implementing them in manageable chunks. For example, an organization can begin by assessing the environment for safety and implementing strategies to promote safety and then focus on subsequent process elements from there.

CONCLUSION

Although there are many concrete practices and strategies necessary to conduct trauma-informed assessment with children and adolescents, these are insufficient unless they are couched within the context of a larger trauma-informed practice approach. Each of the essential practice elements needs to be implemented on top of a foundation that provides support and safety for the family, training and coaching for the clinician who is conducting the assessment, and processes for using the assessment information in a meaningful way. It can be challenging to create a process that includes all of the elements introduced in this chapter, but each of these elements plays a key role in ensuring that the practices highlighted throughout the rest of this book are sustained over time. Whereas this chapter has focused on key principles and essential organizational process elements, the next chapter provides an overview of the assessment process itself and highlights the key domains of a comprehensive trauma-informed assessment process.

3 IMPLEMENTING A COMPREHENSIVE TRAUMA-INFORMED ASSESSMENT

Conducting a comprehensive trauma-informed assessment is a critical step in identifying and addressing the range of needs of traumatized children and families and determining the most effective intervention strategies to address these needs (Kisiel, Blaustein, et al., 2009; Kisiel, Torgersen, et al., 2018). In Chapter 1, we outlined a framework for trauma-informed assessment. In Chapter 2, we introduced the key principles of trauma-informed assessment and essential process elements that need to be in place at the organizational level. In discussing the implementation of trauma-informed assessment, this chapter addresses some additional, individual-level aspects of this framework, including the comprehensive nature of this process and the structure needed for gathering and integrating assessment information so that it can be useful in practice, presenting overarching domains and questions for the clinician to consider. The chapter then details the key domains of a comprehensive trauma-informed assessment; these key domains include the various content areas to assess related to the child, caregiver, and family and their history, responses, and functioning. It also

https://doi.org/10.1037/0000233-003
Trauma-Informed Assessment With Children and Adolescents: Strategies to Support Clinicians, by C. Kisiel, T. Fehrenbach, L. Conradi, and L. Weil

highlights techniques, approaches, and perspectives to incorporate into this process.

USE OF A COMPREHENSIVE TRAUMA-INFORMED ASSESSMENT APPROACH IN PRACTICE

The important aspects of a comprehensive trauma-informed assessment approach that are addressed in this chapter include

- assessing for a range of trauma experiences, areas of need, and strengths;
- using a range of assessment techniques or approaches when gathering this information;
- collecting this information from multiple perspectives or informants;
- assessing youth and caregiver responses to trauma over time; and
- balancing the need for accuracy and consistency in the assessment approach with the need for flexibility based on the specific context.

Incorporating a structure for understanding and interpreting assessment information allows for its meaningful use in clinical decision making (Kisiel, Blaustein, et al., 2009; Kisiel, Conradi, et al., 2014). This comprehensive approach is critical as it offers both an initial, comprehensive clinical profile of a child or adolescent and family and a broader picture of how the needs and strengths of the child and family may shift over time in response to treatment or services. It also provides a context for understanding the complex effects of trauma on both children and their families and a road map for guiding the treatment process (Kisiel, Blaustein, et al., 2009).

A review of the literature indicates that a comprehensive trauma-informed assessment ideally captures information across several key domains. For the child or adolescent, these domains include trauma exposure and loss history; adverse and stressful life experiences; developmental history; trauma responses, including posttraumatic stress reactions, complex trauma reactions, functional difficulties and risk behaviors, perceptions and attributions about trauma, and trauma triggers or reminders; subtypes of trauma responses, including complicated grief reactions and disaster responses; and strengths (Ford, 2011; Kisiel, Conradi, et al., 2014; Layne et al., 2017; Nader, 2011; Nader & Salloum, 2011). For the family and caregiver, these domains include trauma and loss history, needs and functioning. These domains are described in more detail later in this chapter. The next section outlines the recommended techniques to incorporate into a comprehensive trauma-informed assessment and the ways the information gathered can be applied to and integrated into clinical practice.

STRUCTURE AND UTILITY OF A COMPREHENSIVE TRAUMA-INFORMED ASSESSMENT

As initially described in Chapter 1, a trauma-informed assessment ideally takes place over the course of at least a few sessions (e.g., two or three) and incorporates a range of techniques or approaches. These techniques or approaches may include a clinical interview; use of standardized tools or measures that are psychometrically sound; behavioral observations of the child, caregiver, and family; and collateral contacts with family members, other providers (e.g., teacher, caseworker), and other key individuals in the youth's life (Conradi et al., 2011; Kisiel, Conradi, et al., 2014).

Using a comprehensive assessment process that captures information on needs and strengths is a critical step in supporting both treatment planning and clinical intervention, as well as facilitating appropriate service recommendations for youth involved in other child-serving settings (e.g., child welfare, juvenile justice; Kisiel et al., 2017). For instance, it is important to identify not only the relevant needs and key issues to target as goals in mental health treatment and other needed services but also the existing strengths and resources for the youth, the caregiver or family system, other services systems, and the community. Identifying specific areas of strengths and resources (across youth, caregiver and family, and community) and determining how to build and use these areas to address needs and facilitate growth and development for the child and family are critical aspects of trauma-informed treatment and services (Griffin et al., 2009; Kisiel et al., 2017).

The gathering of comprehensive information on the range of both needs and strengths provides a framework for understanding the complex effects of trauma on children and caregivers. In addition, this information is useful in supporting engagement and communication with the family about the effects of trauma. For instance, this information can be used to support awareness raising and education about how a youth's trauma experiences may be related to a range of needs or symptoms that the youth may be having, how these traumatic experiences may have impacted various issues the caregiver and family may be facing, and how many of the emotional and behavioral difficulties exhibited by the youth may likely be ways of coping over time with the overwhelming experience of trauma (A. Cook et al., 2005; Habib & Labruna, 2011). It is important to also share information about the youth's, caregiver's, and family's strengths in this context in order to show areas where they are doing well and how these areas of strength, skill, interest, or talent can be further enhanced to facilitate positive coping and to offer support to the child and family. Identified areas of need and strength can then be reviewed with the child and family and used to guide the development of treatment goals, plans, and decisions based on mutually identified areas of need and strength that can support these goals. These issues are discussed in more detail in subsequent chapters.

GATHERING AND CONSOLIDATING ASSESSMENT INFORMATION FOR USE IN PRACTICE

As noted above, conducting a comprehensive trauma-informed assessment involves gathering information from multiple sources and across several key domains. The use of tools and other sources of data (e.g., interviews, behavioral observation) can guide the clinician in this process. Yet the information gathered may not be helpful (and may feel somewhat overwhelming) unless it is integrated in a manner that helps clinicians effectively develop treatment goals and plans and treat the children and families they serve. To guide the gathering and consolidation of information through this process, clinicians are encouraged to consider the following overarching domains and questions (adapted from Center for Child Trauma Assessment and Service Planning, 2015; Chadwick Center for Children and Families, 2009) that map directly onto the key domains for assessment presented in detail in the next section:

- *trauma exposure and loss history*—What types of trauma or loss has the child experienced? How complex or chronic were the trauma experiences? Has the child experienced multiple forms of trauma or loss? Was the trauma experienced on multiple occasions?

- *developmental history*—How does the child's developmental level or challenges influence their reaction to their experiences and the way they will heal from traumatic experiences? How old is the child chronologically? How old is the child developmentally? Consider the child's attachment to important individuals in their life.

- *trauma responses*—What symptoms is the child currently experiencing, and how severe are they? How have these symptoms served the child as a reaction to the trauma they have experienced? What are the current functional difficulties or risk behaviors the child is exhibiting?

- *family and caregiver trauma and loss history and functioning*—How does the family's and caregiver's trauma or loss history impact their ability to support the child? Does the family environment support the child or create additional stress for them? Do the family and caregiver have particular needs or challenges that may impede their ability to support the child? Specifically, how do the family, social support system, community, and cultural system influence the child?

- *strengths*—What strengths and resources does the child exhibit? What strengths do the caregiver and family bring to the table? What strengths or resources exist in the community? How have these strengths been used in the face of adversity?

Taken together, these overarching domains of assessment can assist clinicians in creating a picture of the child and family, including their unique needs or challenges as well as strengths, to inform the treatment process. More details on the types of questions to consider in relation to specific domain areas are included in Table 3.1. Use of this range of assessment information to inform treatment goals and plans is addressed more fully in Chapter 6. The next section describes the key domains or content areas to assess through this comprehensive process in relation to the child and family or caregiver.

TABLE 3.1. Areas for Consideration in Trauma-Informed Assessment, by Key Domain

Domain	Areas for consideration
Child's trauma exposure and loss history, child's developmental history	• What traumatic events or losses have occurred? • Has the child experienced multiple forms of trauma? • How chronic and severe were the child's trauma experiences? • Is the child still experiencing the trauma? • At what age and developmental stage did the child experience the traumatic events? • What are the other relevant trauma circumstances (e.g., duration and frequency of trauma, relationship to perpetrator, reactions of others following disclosure)?
Trauma responses	
Posttraumatic stress symptoms	• What are the effects of the trauma on current functioning? • What symptoms is the child currently experiencing, and how severe are they? • Is the child exhibiting intrusive thoughts? avoidance? negative changes in thoughts and mood? reexperiencing of the event? changes in baseline level of arousal or reactivity?

(continues)

TABLE 3.1. Areas for Consideration in Trauma-Informed Assessment, by Key Domain (*Continued*)

Domain	Areas for consideration

Complex trauma reactions	• What other trauma-related symptoms or responses is the child exhibiting in addition to or separate from PTSD?
	• How has the trauma affected the following?
	   – ability to form attachments and maintain positive relationships
	   – cognitive processes and learning (e.g., difficulties in sustaining attention, solving problems, or processing information)
	   – ability to regulate mood (e.g., difficulties in modulating emotions, tolerating intense emotions, or labeling and expressing feelings)
	   – behavioral problems (e.g., problems with impulse control, oppositional behaviors)
	   – dissociative symptoms (e.g., problems with blanking or spacing out, persistent forgetfulness, alterations or shifts in consciousness)
	   – physiological responses (e.g., difficulty regulating bodily functions, including sleeping, eating, and elimination)

Functional difficulties and risk behaviors	• What is the child's social history? • How many close friends does the child have? • How does the child do in school? • How does the child spend recreational or free time? • Does the child have experiences with bullying? gang involvement? substance abuse? • Are there additional risk behaviors? • What is the child's education history? Has the child ever received special education services or an individualized education plan? Are there any other educational-related concerns?
Complicated grief reactions[a]	• What is the child's relationship or attachment to the deceased individual? • What are the grief reactions and difficulties the child is manifesting in response to the loss? • Are the grief reactions persistent or prolonged (i.e., for more than a year)?
Disaster responses[a]	• Did the child experience a disaster, were they near a disaster, or did they lose a loved one in a disaster? • Does the child have specific needs, life disruptions, or secondary adversities related to the disaster?

TABLE 3.1. Areas for Consideration in Trauma-Informed Assessment, by Key Domain (*Continued*)

Domain	Areas for consideration
Trauma triggers and reminders	• Are there specific triggers or reminders for the child (e.g., based on sight, smell, or touch) that prompt or worsen heightened responses? • Is the child or caregiver aware of these triggers and reminders?
Perceptions and attributions	• How does the child perceive the causes of the traumatic event? Does the child consider self or others to blame? • How do these perceptions and attributions about the trauma relate to the child's coping responses?
Family and caregiver trauma and loss history, family and caregiver functioning	• What is the family's history of trauma, substance abuse, and mental health problems? • Was the child exposed to substances in utero? • What is the child's relationship with caregivers, siblings, and other family members? • How is the family system functioning overall? • What are the caregiver's perceptions and attributions and coping responses to the trauma?
Strengths of the child, caregiver, and community	• What are the child's, caregiver's, and family's strengths and resources within the broader community? • How can these strengths be supported and strengthened and used to improve the child's functioning and resilience?

Note. ᵃFor the specific areas of complicated grief and disaster responses, potential screening questions are listed to determine whether the child was impacted by these events. If responses are positive, the child may require referral for a more in-depth assessment specific to a complicated grief reaction or disaster response.
From "Assessing the Effects of Trauma in Children and Adolescents in Practice Settings," by C. Kisiel, L. Conradi, T. Fehrenbach, E. Torgersen, and E. C. Briggs, 2014, *Journal of Child and Adolescent Psychiatric Clinics of North America, 23*(2), p. 226 (https://doi.org/10.1016/j.chc.2013.12.007). Copyright 2014 by Elsevier. Adapted with permission.

KEY DOMAINS OF A TRAUMA-INFORMED ASSESSMENT

When conducting a comprehensive trauma-informed assessment with children and adolescents, it is essential to assess for a wide range of traumatic events and relevant experiences and history, the impact of these experiences across domains of functioning, and areas of strength (Kisiel, Conradi, et al., 2014). This comprehensive picture will help guide the most effective treatment plan and intervention process for children and families impacted by trauma. This section details the key domains to assess through this comprehensive process, with areas for consideration in each domain. In addition, Table 3.1 provides additional questions for consideration in the context of assessing these areas (see Kisiel, Conradi, et al., 2014, for further details). Note that these questions are meant to inform the clinical interview process, interviews with other providers, case conceptualization, and treatment planning efforts. Specific assessment tools in relation to these domains are reviewed in Chapter 5.

Trauma Exposure and Loss History

It is important to consider the traumatic events experienced by children and adolescents when conducting a trauma-informed assessment. When assessing traumatic events, considering a broad range of events is important. Types of traumatic events include (but are not limited to) the following:

- child abuse or maltreatment (including physical abuse, sexual abuse, emotional abuse, and neglect),
- domestic violence and family violence,
- medical trauma (including chronic illness and repeated surgeries),
- community violence,
- school violence and bullying,
- refugee and war trauma,
- traumatic loss,
- disasters (natural and anthropogenic),
- car accidents and other types of serious accidents (e.g., in the home or community), and
- exposure to terrorist acts.

In addition, when assessing traumatic experiences, it is important to consider the circumstances surrounding the traumatic events as these may impact youth responses to trauma (Nader, 2008b). For instance, clinicians should consider whether the trauma experiences were single events or repeated or chronic trauma experiences and the cumulative impact of several different trauma experiences; chronic and cumulative trauma potentially lead to different outcomes as indicated by an extensive literature published over the past several decades (Herman, 1992; Nader, 2008b; Terr, 1991). Other key exposure characteristics to consider include the severity of the trauma experiences (e.g., whether violence or injury was involved), the age of onset or developmental stage at which the trauma occurred, the duration of the trauma (number of months or years over which it occurred), the youth's relationship to the perpetrator, whether the youth disclosed the trauma, and to what degree the youth was believed and supported when disclosing the trauma (Claussen & Crittenden, 1991; Hodgdon et al., 2018; McGee et al., 1997; Nader, 2008b). All of these areas can impact the short- and long-term outcomes for youth following exposure to trauma. These circumstances are addressed in more detail in other publications (Claussen & Crittenden, 1991; Hodgdon et al., 2018; McGee et al., 1997). Additional questions for consideration in this regard are listed in Table 3.1.

Further, there is a large and growing body of literature on the pervasive impact of *complex trauma exposure*, which includes chronic and multiple trauma exposures that are interpersonal in nature, often by caregivers and beginning at an early age. Complex trauma experiences can have a unique impact across several domains of development and functioning (A. Cook et al., 2005; Greeson et al., 2011; Kisiel, Fehrenbach, et al., 2009).

Adverse and Stressful Life Experiences

In addition to assessing for trauma exposure, it is important to gather information on a broader set of adverse or stressful life experiences as well. An important study related to child trauma assessment is the Adverse Childhood Experiences (ACE) Study (Felitti et al., 1998). The ACE Study has played a pivotal role in increasing our understanding of the linkage between childhood adversity and long-term health outcomes in adults (see Appendix A for more information on this study).

As described in Chapter 1, in addition to examining a range of trauma experiences, the ACE Study also included a broader range of stressful life experiences, including parental or caregiver substance abuse, mental illness, criminal behavior, and separation or divorce (Felitti et al., 1998). Assessing for secondary adversities that may result from trauma exposure or other stressful life events may be important in understanding the context of the youth and family. These adversities may include the challenges that can result from removal from the home and relocation to a new neighborhood or school setting because of trauma. Additional stressors include parental job loss or financial hardship and system-induced traumas (e.g., for youth involved in child welfare or juvenile justice), such as multiple foster placements, sibling separation, and use of seclusions or restraints.

Developmental History

It is essential to gather some information on the child's developmental history and functioning prior to their trauma exposures (if possible). This information can include an account of when and how the child achieved key developmental milestones (e.g., cognitive development, social and emotional development, fine and gross motor skill development, speech and language development). For instance, it is useful to have some understanding of whether the child had any prior challenges or delays across these developmental domains and whether exposure to trauma further impacted the achievement of milestones or skills within any of these areas. Facing developmental challenges or delays over the course of a child's life can also contribute to ongoing stress and exacerbate responses to trauma (De Bellis & Zisk, 2014; Perry et al., 1995).

Trauma Responses

This section details the various types of trauma responses to assess among youth, indicates how these responses can manifest, and provides a brief rationale for why it is important to assess these areas.

Posttraumatic Stress Reactions

When assessing for posttraumatic stress disorder (PTSD) or reactions, it is important to consider both the diagnosis of PTSD and its various symptom manifestations, including reexperiencing or intrusive symptoms, avoidance of trauma-related stimuli (thoughts, feelings, or reminders), increased arousal and reactivity, and negative alterations in cognitions and mood (American Psychiatric Association, 2013). This consideration is important as many youth manifest certain symptoms of PTSD but may not meet full diagnostic criteria. Rather, youth in particular may be more likely to have a broad range of responses to trauma, including but not limited to the symptom clusters of PTSD (Ackerman et al., 1998; A. Cook et al., 2005; Kisiel, Fehrenbach, et al., 2009). This fact further suggests the critical importance of using a comprehensive assessment framework when conducting assessments with youth impacted by trauma, as assessing for PTSD alone can often lead to missing key domains that may be impacted by trauma (Kisiel, Fehrenbach, et al., 2014).

As Dalenberg and Briere (2017) noted, PTSD is often the primary emphasis of the trauma assessment process; however, exposure to trauma is a risk factor for the development of several mental health difficulties, and PTSD is only one possible outcome (Boney-McCoy & Finkelhor, 1995; Newman, 2014) that may not manifest in all youth impacted by trauma (Kisiel, Fehrenbach, et al., 2009, 2014). Therefore, using a broader framework in the assessment of trauma among youth is critical.

Complex Trauma Reactions

Many children and adolescents exhibit a broader range of traumatic stress symptoms that extend beyond the primary symptoms associated with PTSD. Given that PTSD symptoms capture only a limited aspect of posttraumatic responses among youth (Nader, 2011; van der Kolk & Courtois, 2005), assessing for a broader range of responses is equally important (Kisiel, Fehrenbach, et al., 2014; Nader, 2011). Complex trauma reactions have been described as including manifestations of impaired self-dysregulation across several areas or domains of functioning, including affect or emotional dysregulation (e.g., difficulty recognizing or expressing emotions or modulating intense emotions), cognitive dysregulation (e.g., problems with attention, memory, or encoding information), behavioral dysregulation (e.g., problems with goal-directed behavior or aggressive or impulsive behavior), relational dysregulation (e.g., problems with forming attachments with caregivers or other important adults; difficulties with peer relationships), bodily dysregulation (e.g., somatic difficulties, physical health problems), and dissociation (A. Cook et al., 2005; Ford, 2011). This complex trauma framework can also help explain functional difficulties and risk behaviors, as further described next.

Functional Difficulties and Risk Behaviors

Complex trauma responses can lead to or exacerbate functional impairment across several key areas (Ford, 2011). These areas are important to assess as they impact a youth's day-to-day functioning, and they include problems with relationships with primary caregivers, peers, and social functioning more broadly; information processing (attention and concentration, memory and executive functions); impulse control and risk-taking behaviors (with implications for safety and legal involvement); and school or work functioning (Ford, 2011). Other functional difficulties include problems with developmental or intellectual functioning, sexual development and behavior, medical or physical well-being and functioning, and participation in recreational activities. In addition, the assessment should address risk behaviors such as physical or sexual aggression, suicidal or self-harm behaviors, delinquency, fire setting, and substance abuse (A. Cook et al., 2005; Kisiel, Fehrenbach, et al., 2009).

Perceptions and Attributions About Trauma

Gathering information on youths' attributions about their trauma experiences (e.g., whether they consider themselves or others to blame) is important as this allows clinicians to gain a better sense of their experience of the trauma. *Attributions* are inferences about the cause of traumatic events, other situations, or actions. Collins and colleagues (2013) found that exposure to trauma negatively impacted children's perceptions about these events and that negative attributions were associated with more trauma symptoms overall. Further, several studies have suggested that children's attributions in relation to their trauma experiences can also have a significant impact on subsequent trauma symptoms (Collins et al., 2013, 2017; Knight & Sullivan, 2006). These studies indicate that children who have an attributional style that is internal (e.g., blames self for causing the event to happen), stable (e.g., considers the event inevitable or constant), and global (e.g., believes the event to be generalizable to other aspects of life) are more likely to experience negative psychological outcomes (Collins et al., 2017; Deblinger & Runyon, 2005; Knight & Sullivan, 2006).

Some common negative attributions found among children impacted by trauma include self-blame, distrust of others, feeling different from peers, and feeling a lack of credibility (Collins et al., 2017; Mannarino et al., 1994). These findings indicate that the explanation or reason children identify for the occurrence of their trauma experiences significantly impacts their ability to cope with these experiences. Therefore, understanding youths' perceptions of and attributions about their trauma can help clinicians further identify their coping styles and the meaning of their symptom patterns and responses; this understanding can assist clinicians in addressing these issues in the context of treatment (see Collins et al., 2013, 2017, for more information).

Trauma Triggers or Reminders

In addition to gathering information on trauma exposure and other relevant history, the trauma-informed assessment process includes identifying circumstances that may trigger trauma-related responses. A *trauma trigger or reminder* is a stimulus that acts as a reminder of a traumatic event that occurred and can lead to a set of emotional or behavioral responses that are designed to help the youth cope with these traumatic experiences in the present (van der Kolk, 1998). Sometimes triggers are obvious or clearly identified in relation to a child's trauma experiences, such as sexual situations, unexpected touching by others, loud noises, close proximity to the event, or arguments between others (Fallot & Harris, 2001). However, some triggers are less obvious, and these triggers may be either consciously or unconsciously connected to the trauma experiences (van der Kolk, 1998). Nonetheless, it is useful for the clinician to identify and explore potential triggers with both the youth and caregiver in order to better understand the youth's responses to trauma. The youth and caregiver can learn to identify these triggers early on with the intention of building healthier or more effective emotional and behavioral responses when triggers arise over time.

Subtypes of Trauma Response
In addition to the range of trauma responses described above, it is important to consider some unique patterns of trauma responses that often occur in relation to particular types of trauma exposure. Described next are two of the more widely researched subtypes of trauma response, complicated grief reactions and disaster responses, with suggested areas to consider in the assessment of youth impacted by these types of trauma.

Complicated Grief Reactions. Whereas normal grief reactions to loss are associated with a range of short-term difficulties in youth (e.g., internalizing and externalizing symptoms, increased risk for illness, academic difficulties), there are several factors that may complicate the grieving process. These factors include the importance of the relationship with the deceased individual, the potentially traumatic nature of the loss, and the presence of other disturbances in combination with the grief (Nader, 2011; Nader & Salloum, 2011; Pearlman et al., 2014). Complicated grief reactions may be cumulative and include a continuous set of possible reactions. The primary types of complicated grief reactions include *traumatic grief,* which relates to a death that occurs in a traumatic way and may include trauma reactions that interfere with adaptive grieving (Nader & Salloum, 2011), and *prolonged grief,* which includes normal grief symptoms that are persistent and exacerbated, with an emphasis on the attachment to the deceased (Boelen et al., 2006; Prigerson et al., 2009). Given that these manifestations of grief may be distinct, it is important to assess for these and the related circumstances in addition to the other potential trauma reactions that youth may be exhibiting. Table 3.1 lists some initial questions to consider when determining whether complicated grief reactions are present; the answers may suggest the need for more detailed assessment this area.

Disaster Responses. An additional targeted but important area of trauma-informed assessment is related to children's disaster responses. A framework for child disaster mental health assessment has been proposed over the past decade for use by providers in a variety of settings (Pfefferbaum et al., 2012). This framework includes assessment of both individual and community needs, as both are essential components of disaster response. There are several levels of disaster screening and assessment, including broader community-level assessment (e.g., needs assessment, monitoring and surveillance of community-based needs, program evaluation), screening of the population of youth impacted by a disaster within a community, and clinical evaluation of individual youth (Pfefferbaum et al., 2012). The clinical evaluation process for individual youth is akin to the child- and family-level trauma-informed assessment discussed in this book; this process involves in-depth assessment of youth (and family members) who are directly exposed to a disaster and identified as being at risk for psychiatric difficulties. A full diagnostic assessment (including but not limited to PTSD) is provided with the goal of identifying psychopathology and the need for different levels of clinical care (e.g., mental health treatment, psychosocial interventions; Pfefferbaum & North, 2013, 2016). It is useful to consider this type of assessment for youth exposed to any disaster, terrorist attack, or other mass trauma event (Pfefferbaum et al., 2012). Table 3.1 lists initial questions to consider when determining whether there is a need for a more detailed disaster-related clinical evaluation; readers should also refer to the citations in this section for more information.

Family and Caregiver Trauma and Loss History

Assessing for relevant areas of family and caregiver history is also important in understanding the context of a youth's trauma responses. This area of assessment can provide an understanding of caregiver or family exposure to trauma or loss (e.g., trauma in childhood or adulthood, partner violence, domestic violence, traumatic loss). This area can also reveal patterns of trauma exposure in the family or community that are repeated across generations (e.g., community violence, family violence, ongoing loss of family members). The assessment process can include gathering information on other adverse experiences or additional stressors that may arise in relation to trauma or loss, such as financial difficulties, job loss, or homelessness. A family or caregiver history of trauma may compound the impact of the youth's trauma experiences for the youth, caregiver, and other family members.

Family and Caregiver Needs and Functioning

In addition to the family and caregiver trauma history, it is important to gather information on caregiver or family needs and functioning both in response to trauma and also more broadly. For instance, in relation to the family and caregiver trauma history described above, family members may experience their own posttraumatic symptoms, a broad range of other mental health symptoms (e.g., anxiety, depression, substance abuse), and potential triggers in response to either their own trauma history or that of their children. Understanding and assessing the mental health challenges or functional difficulties of caregivers and other family members (whether related to their trauma history or not) is important as they may impact the caregiver's or family's ability to support the child in the context of the child's needs.

Family and caregiver needs or challenges can have an impact on caregiving capacity more broadly, particularly as they relate to the caregivers' ability to support the child in understanding and addressing the impact of the child's trauma and loss history and supporting the child's process of recovery. Some key areas to assess in this regard include the caregiver's knowledge of the youth and the youth's areas of difficulty, the caregiver's understanding of the youth's potential trauma triggers, and the caregiver's ability to support the child in navigating these triggers and building more effective and healthy coping strategies. An important part of assessment involves identifying caregivers' ability to support, care for, and supervise the child and to organize and facilitate involvement in the range of services needed. It is also important to identify the caregiver's perception of their child's trauma, the caregiver's attributions about the child's experiences, and the caregiver's own coping responses to the trauma of their child. In addition, if any of the caregivers' responses are affecting or impeding the child's recovery process, it may be important for the therapist to address this concern with the caregiver or make a referral for support services for the caregiver.

Strengths: Child, Caregiver, and Community

It is essential for clinicians conducting trauma-informed assessment to take a whole-person approach that emphasizes the child's and family's strengths and resources in addition to their areas of need (Fallot & Harris, 2001). Focusing on strengths within the child, caregiver, and community in the context of the assessment process is critical as evidence has indicated that building strengths and resilience is one critical pathway for reducing the impact of and promoting recovery from the effects of trauma (Griffin et al., 2009; Kisiel et al., 2017). Assessment of the specific strengths or skills of the child can include areas such as interpersonal skills, academic skills and mastery, creative talents and interests, extracurricular skills and interests, self-esteem and self-confidence, and spiritual or religious interests or sense of meaning or purpose (Fallot & Harris, 2001; Kisiel et al., 2017).

It is equally important to assess the strengths and resources within the child's caregiver and family system and community, such as sources of social support or social assets, financial support or stability, and ability to support the child in obtaining the services needed not only to address their trauma but also to build additional areas of skill or strength. Beyond the immediate caregiver and family system, it is also useful to identify whether there are other areas of support, strengths, and resources within the child's community or within other systems that the child may be involved with (Griffin et al., 2009; Kisiel et al., 2017). Ideally, these identified resources or strengths will be integrated into treatment plans as areas to build on as the youth, caregiver, and family work to further enhance areas of strength and positive coping strategies in order to improve youth functioning and support the process of recovery from trauma overall.

ASSESSING AND UNDERSTANDING DIAGNOSES IN THE CONTEXT OF TRAUMA-INFORMED ASSESSMENT

Although a diagnostic assessment is not typically incorporated as part of comprehensive trauma-informed assessment (rather, it may be included in a general mental health assessment or a comprehensive psychological evaluation), some recommendations and suggestions are listed here for clinicians who may conduct a diagnostic assessment as part of this process. Diagnostic assessment may occur, for instance, when a trauma-informed assessment is conducted as part of a broader intake assessment process in which diagnostic assessment also takes place or when a diagnostic assessment needs to occur as a mandate for a funding source.

Assessing for mental health diagnoses can be complicated for youth impacted by trauma, given the diverse symptoms that children may manifest across the key domains and trauma responses described above. Furthermore, overlapping symptoms exist across disorders that may make differential diagnosis difficult (Nader, 2008b). Studies focused on PTSD assessment highlight the extensive comorbidity with other diagnoses, emphasizing the range of conditions and disorders that can accompany PTSD, including depression and anxiety disorders, attention-deficit/hyperactivity disorder, substance abuse, oppositional defiant disorder, and conduct disorders (Fallot & Harris, 2001; Newman, 2014; Newman et al., 1996). This comorbidity can make the process of differential diagnosis challenging for clinicians. However, one recommendation (in relation to the *Diagnostic and Statistical Manual of Mental Disorders* [*DSM*], fourth edition; American Psychiatric

Association, 1994) suggests that when a PTSD diagnosis does exist (and when symptoms are directly related to the PTSD Criterion A exposure), this PTSD diagnosis may supersede other diagnoses when possible (Nader, 2008b). However, this recommendation is not always readily followed in practice, perhaps given the range of other symptom manifestations and potential diagnoses that may be of pressing concern and that need to be addressed in the context of treatment as well. One of the benefits of a comprehensive trauma-informed assessment process using the key domains described above is that it can help tease out diagnoses more effectively on the basis of the range of trauma and loss experiences, symptom patterns, and functional difficulties and other areas of concern identified.

However, because of the range of possible responses to trauma, there is a likely possibility of multiple diagnoses for youth impacted by trauma. Given that many of these diagnoses fail to take into consideration the trauma and its impact, the potential for treating these conditions in isolation and for mislabeling and underestimating trauma-related symptoms poses a significant concern (Fallot & Harris, 2001; van der Kolk, 2005). Therefore, using a comprehensive trauma-informed assessment process is critical to help providers and family members understand the range of possible trauma-related symptoms and diagnoses (when identified), to support trauma-informed treatment plans, and to facilitate psychoeducation and collaboration with families and other providers about the wide-ranging impacts of trauma. This process of translating assessment findings to practice is addressed in more detail in Chapter 6.

USING MULTIPLE REPORTERS AND A RANGE OF ASSESSMENT TECHNIQUES

When gathering information across the key domains listed above, it is important for clinicians to attempt to collect this information from a variety of key adults in the youth's life, including primary caregivers, other key family members, teachers, and other providers involved in the child's care. Gathering information from primary caregivers is typically done in the context of a clinical interview, through use of standardized tools, and during behavioral observation with the child and caregiver, as described below. In addition, it is recommended that information be gathered from other key adults, including family members who play an important role in the child's life (e.g., aunt or uncle, grandparents) and other providers based on services the child receives (e.g., teacher, tutor) or systems they are involved in (e.g., caseworker, probation officer).

Collateral interviews or meetings with family members and other service providers (by phone or in person) are typically used to gather additional assessment information. These collateral contacts may involve the use of standardized tools (e.g., provider report tools) or collection of less structured information on the child's functioning within the different settings. Family members and other providers may be asked to share feedback on how the child is doing generally or in relation to particular areas of concern for the child within particular settings. These assessment techniques are discussed in more detail in Chapter 5. This feedback is important as youth may behave differently based on the setting or the adults they interact with, and therefore unique challenges and strengths for the youth may emerge in these different contexts; this is useful to be aware of as clinicians develop their treatment plans and understand the full picture of the child (Kisiel, Conradi, et al., 2014; Kisiel, Torgersen, et al., 2018). The process of collaborating with other providers and developing treatment plans based on assessment information is discussed in more detail in Chapter 6.

It is critical to use a range of assessment techniques when conducting a comprehensive trauma-informed assessment, including but not limited to standardized tools (e.g., that tap into the range of key domains and from the perspective of different reporters), clinical interviews, collateral interviews, and behavioral observations. These techniques have strengths and weaknesses, which is why it is important to use this multifaceted approach. Assessment measures come in a variety of formats including child self-report or caregiver report (e.g., paper-and-pencil) tools, provider report tools, and semistructured diagnostic tools. Many types of assessment tools exist, each offering unique benefits and challenges. A comprehensive assessment generally incorporates tools completed by multiple informants in order to gather the most complete picture of the child based on a range of perspectives (Conradi et al., 2011; Kisiel, Conradi, et al., 2014). Various types of tools are described in more detail in Chapter 5.

A clinical interview has the advantage of being a flexible approach that can enhance engagement and understanding of the child and family, allowing the clinician a greater ability to translate and rephrase various questions. This interview is a key part of the assessment process as it offers the opportunity to gather open-ended information on the range of domains described above; it can also support and enhance the information collected through standardized tools. Yet there may be limits to the accuracy of information gathered during the clinical interview; for instance, the youth may not be comfortable sharing certain information directly, particularly at the outset of services (e.g., during an initial assessment) when a relationship is not yet established with the clinician (Newman, 2014).

In the clinical interview, it is recommended that the clinician take great care and be sensitive to the range of personal information being gathered during the trauma-informed assessment process, recognizing that youth may be less willing to share in this manner, especially if being asked about this information for the first time. For instance, before asking a youth directly about their trauma experiences, it may be useful to initially gather this sensitive information from caregivers and other providers (e.g., a caseworker) who know the youth and are familiar with their trauma experiences and history or their current difficulties. This strategy may minimize some of these challenges and also allow the youth to feel more at ease with the clinician already knowing some of these details. The information gathered can be shared with the youth in the interest of transparency and to support engagement between the clinician and youth, relying on the youth for further clarification as needed and for sharing of new information (e.g., traumas unknown to adult caregivers or providers). Further, it is recommended that the clinician make the youth aware of the concerns that are identified in the assessment process, as well as the youth's strengths, so that these issues can be discussed openly. These details should always be communicated to the youth in a developmentally sensitive and appropriate manner.

Finally, it is important to consider behavioral observations of the child and family during this process, including body language, emotional and behavioral responses, and what the child chooses to share or not share. These observations can all offer insight into the youth's coping responses, perceptions or attributions about their trauma experiences, and receptivity to receiving help. Observations of the youth and family members together also offers useful information on family dynamics, relationships, and functioning (e.g., in terms of how family members relate when discussing trauma experiences). This may manifest, for instance, as family members becoming overly protective of or overinvolved with a child following their experiences of trauma. Sharing feedback on these observed dynamics with family members can help inform and support the treatment process.

Because of the range of techniques and multiple reporters used in the comprehensive assessment process, discrepant information is likely to arise. For example, different reporters may characterize the child's functioning differently, including specific areas of need, the severity of needs, and areas of strength. The child's needs may also manifest differently across settings, or certain reporters (including the child) may be more or less willing to identify or acknowledge the range of needs. It is not uncommon, for instance, for the child's and caregiver's reports of symptoms to have some discrepancies. It is the clinician's job to help make sense of these inconsistencies and to use them as an opportunity for communication, collaboration, and enhanced understanding among members of the family and other providers when appropriate (Kisiel, Conradi, et al., 2014). Integrating this comprehensive assessment information in the context of establishing treatment goals and collaborative treatment planning with children and families is the next critical step, described in Chapter 6.

CHALLENGES WITH USING A COMPREHENSIVE TRAUMA-INFORMED ASSESSMENT APPROACH

There are times when the comprehensive assessment approach described in this chapter is not fully realistic for clinicians to use in their practice settings given staff time or resource constraints (e.g., staff capacity, cost of certain tools). For instance, it may not always be feasible to gather information across all of the key domains or in as much detail as noted above. Therefore, it is important to note that these recommendations are considered the "ideal" process, which is more achievable when there are no significant time constraints on completing the assessment process. However, the reality may be that assessments have to be completed more quickly than preferred, given the constraints that may exist with insurance coverage for trauma-informed assessments (e.g., some policies cover a limited number of assessment-focused sessions) and other time constraints or demands in clinical practice settings. Some practical solutions to these challenges are described in the section that follows.

In addition, given the complex and varied responses that youth often have to trauma, particularly following exposure to chronic or complex trauma, there may be issues with diagnostic comorbidity and making differential diagnoses. There may also be challenges associated with potentially misdiagnosing or mislabeling youth who have symptoms of complex trauma, particularly if the information is not gathered across various domains in the context of a comprehensive trauma-informed assessment process. Misdiagnosis or mislabeling also may occur if information is gathered only on PTSD symptoms or if other potential symptom manifestations (e.g., inattention, depression, oppositionality, conduct symptoms) are identified but not linked as part of the trauma response when they are, in fact, related to a youth's experience of trauma.

Furthermore, if training or consultation is not offered to support making connections among the broad range of potential responses or symptom patterns and their relationship to a youth's trauma experiences, there may be issues with understanding these linkages or treating these symptoms in isolation (Kisiel, Fehrenbach, et al., 2014; Kisiel, Patterson, et al., 2018).

Issues of potential mislabeling and misdiagnosis may also be compounded by the current absence of an established diagnostic framework in the *DSM* that captures the broad range of potential trauma reactions and diagnoses associated with complex trauma in children (D'Andrea et al., 2012; Denton et al., 2017). As a result, there may be a greater potential for these youth to receive multiple mental health diagnoses given their varied symptom manifestations; it is then the challenge and responsibility of the clinician to make linkages, when appropriate, between a youth's trauma experiences and these various diagnoses as potential responses to trauma.

Finally, although the suggested comprehensive trauma-informed assessment approach and techniques described above have several beneficial practice implications, more empirical evidence is needed to establish the overall utility of the approach and how using it may improve practice with or outcomes for youth and families. Certain aspects of this comprehensive approach have been evaluated; for example, incorporating standardized assessment tools into routine practice has been associated with improved outcomes for youth as well as adults (e.g., Bickman et al., 2011; J. R. Cook et al., 2017), and there is evidence that client engagement and outcomes are improved when diagnoses identified through the assessment (e.g., standardized interview) match those identified by the clinician (Jensen-Doss & Weisz, 2008). More research is needed to fully assess the utility and impact associated with using all aspects of this comprehensive trauma-informed assessment approach.

PRACTICAL STRATEGIES AND CONSIDERATIONS FOR CLINICIANS

Below are some practical strategies and tips to help clinicians gather the most critical details during a trauma-informed assessment. These are adapted based on an earlier publication (Kisiel, Conradi, et al., 2014) and are listed in terms of overall considerations and in relation to the challenges described in this chapter:

1. Focus on orienting the youth and family to the assessment process (e.g., purpose, overview of process, what you plan to cover) and determining their key concerns. This modest investment can not only enhance engagement but also help guide attention to the most pressing issues.

2. To help address the time constraints you may face in conducting a comprehensive assessment (and potential constraints with insurance coverage for multiple assessment sessions), consider having the caregiver

and youth complete some tools before arriving for their session. Some options include using technology to make these tools accessible, sending some tools in advance as part of the clinic package, and having the caregiver and youth complete some tools in the waiting room prior to or after their appointment. If this strategy is used, make sure to have a thoughtful process to introduce the caregiver and youth to why they are completing the tools and how the information will be used.

3. Check in with the youth, caregiver, and other family members regarding initial impressions and hypotheses related to areas of concern for the youth. This can be done to ensure that any critical concerns are not being missed or to see if they have different ideas or interpretations of the key issues. Many will feel validated by this experience and will appreciate the opportunity to actively partner in the youth's care. As a part of this process, consider gathering anecdotal feedback from families on how this assessment process improved their buy-in, connection, or understanding of the assessment process as meaningful and share this feedback with your clinical team to determine which assessment practices are most useful to adopt within your setting.

4. When time is limited, focus on the most pressing issues or concerns first, as identified in collaboration with the family. Work in conjunction with your clinical supervisor as needed (or with other staff who can support this work) to identify the techniques and tools to use initially in gathering key information within the limited time frame. Then complete the most relevant tools (based on the referral questions) at the outset. For instance, consider what is possible to do if one session is the initial time frame allocated for assessment. Even within this shorter time frame, consider incorporating at least a few different techniques, such as some open-ended questions (i.e., as a part of a clinical interview), observation, and use of one or more measures (described further in Chapter 5). Consider asking the caregiver and youth to complete relevant tools before or after the in-person assessment sessions.

5. Set the expectation for an ongoing assessment process up front as it will be easier to continue to gather additional information across the multiple assessment domains over time, even with these constraints (as described in Chapter 2). This ongoing assessment information can continue to be integrated into the process of treatment planning and goal setting. Further, when information is gathered as part of a follow-up assessment, it can be used to monitor progress over time (e.g., to understand symptom reduction and strengths building throughout treatment) and help inform modifications to treatment goals or plans.

6. Consider offering staff trainings or facilitating discussions in clinical team meetings to increase staff knowledge and skill in understanding complex trauma, integrating the variety of information gathered across key domains, and determining how it may relate to diagnostic overlap or comorbidity or potential issues of mislabeling or misdiagnosis. Offer support and education to fellow clinicians about how to integrate this information and translate it into meaningful treatment goals and plans in collaboration with youth, caregivers, and families (Kisiel, Conradi, et al., 2014; Kisiel, Torgersen, et al., 2018). Integration of assessment results into practice is discussed in detail in Chapter 6.

CONCLUSION

There are several important areas to consider in a comprehensive trauma-informed assessment, including assessing for a range of trauma experiences and areas of need and strength; using a range of techniques and multiple perspectives to collect this information; gathering assessment information both initially and over time; collecting detailed information while also maintaining a flexible approach that is sensitive to the needs of the youth and family within the context; and organizing this comprehensive information so that it can be useful in clinical practice. When gathering information across the key domains, areas to consider include trauma and loss history of the youth, caregiver, and family and the range of symptom manifestations, functional difficulties, coping responses, and perceptions about the trauma for both youth and caregivers. Equally important to consider are areas of strengths and resources that can support youth on their path to recovery.

Although the recommended comprehensive approach and suggested domains for assessment are multifaceted, clinicians need to balance them with the practical reality that time and resources for conducting an assessment in this manner are not always available. Therefore, clinicians need to be willing to adopt a flexible approach when conducting a trauma-informed assessment, always prioritizing the needs of the youth and family and considering ways to use the assessment information gathered to support the treatment process and enhance the strengths and resilience of the youth and family. Chapter 4 emphasizes the importance of a flexible approach to trauma-informed assessment, with a focus on adapting the assessment process to fit the individual developmental and sociocultural context of youth and families.

4

TAILORING THE TRAUMA-INFORMED ASSESSMENT TO THE DEVELOPMENTAL AND SOCIOCULTURAL CONTEXT OF THE CHILD AND FAMILY

Earlier chapters provided concrete recommendations regarding the structure and process of trauma-informed assessment with children and youth. This chapter focuses on the importance of structuring and adapting the assessment protocol and process to best fit the individual developmental and sociocultural context of the youth and families clinicians serve. In this chapter, *sociocultural context* refers to the range of developmental, societal, and cultural variables that may influence an individual's exposure and responses to, interpretation of, and recovery from traumatic events. Such variables include but are not limited to race, ethnicity, religion, economic status, cultural values and beliefs, and immigration status.

The information in this chapter is drawn from a modest body of literature on culturally sensitive trauma-informed assessment (e.g., de Arellano & Danielson, 2008; Hays, 2008; Nader, 2007, 2008a), as well as research and literature about specific populations, specifically young children and adolescents; youth with intellectual or developmental disabilities; system-involved youth and families; lesbian, gay, bisexual, transgender, and queer or questioning (LGBTQ) youth; people of color (POC) and Indigenous people;

https://doi.org/10.1037/0000233-004
Trauma-Informed Assessment With Children and Adolescents: Strategies to Support Clinicians, by C. Kisiel, T. Fehrenbach, L. Conradi, and L. Weil

and immigrants and refugees. This chapter identifies barriers that result when sociocultural context is not attended to; it also provides clinicians with practical recommendations for preventing and addressing these barriers. Ultimately, the purpose of this chapter is to help clinicians reflect on how to conduct trauma-informed assessments in a way that is culturally sensitive, respectful, and responsive.

In an effort to highlight a broad range of sociocultural factors, this chapter is limited in the amount of detail provided on each of the individual topics listed above. Readers are therefore strongly encouraged to examine the reference materials cited throughout this chapter to deepen their knowledge in a given area.

Valuing and responding sensitively to variability in sociocultural context is critical when conducting trauma-informed assessments with children and families. Stated more generally, it is necessary to conceptualize each youth's and family's unique combination of needs and strengths, some of which are a product of their individual personality or character, and many of which are tied directly to the ecological systems within which they exist (Bronfenbrenner, 1992). A sociocultural perspective includes the understanding that family dynamics, community supports, and political climate can all strongly impact the way youth interpret, respond to, and recover from traumatic stress (American Psychological Association, 2018; Chavez-Dueñas et al., 2019). It is necessary for clinicians to attend to these factors throughout the assessment process and to adjust their approach as necessary in order to be responsive to the cultural differences of clients. This culturally responsive approach to assessment requires that clinicians stay curious and humble throughout and that they be willing to recognize and take responsibility for missteps they may unintentionally make along the way.

Research has shown that cultural missteps are common in psychotherapy, that therapists are often unaware when they commit microaggressions, and that these missteps negatively impact the therapeutic alliance (Owen et al., 2014, 2018). Notably, Owen and colleagues (2014) found that even when controlling for the therapist's race and ethnicity, the microaggressions negatively affected the working alliance. Fortunately, studies also show that such missteps and their negative outcomes can be resolved and that relationships can be repaired when microaggressions are openly addressed (Owen et al., 2014). A meta-analysis by Soto et al. (2018) concluded that the client's perception of the therapist's "multicultural competence" was highly predictive of positive therapeutic outcomes, whereas the therapist's own perception of their competence was not. This finding may imply that therapists do not always accurately assess their own cultural competence or that their perception may differ from that of their clients, which speaks to clinicians' need to broaden their knowledge and skill in this area.

Soto and colleagues (2018) also found that "the more cultural adaptations to treatment, the more clinical improvement" clients experience (p. 1919); one could hypothesize that the same may be true for cultural adaptations made to mental health assessment. Ultimately, this extra effort to interact with clients in a culturally responsive way has the potential to positively impact the trauma-informed assessment process by improving trust, rapport, communication, and collaboration with the youth and family, increasing the likelihood that the information they provide is valid and complete and allowing for the development of more accurate, meaningful, and helpful conclusions and recommendations.

The importance of understanding clients within their broader socio-cultural context has been recognized for decades (Falicov, 1988); today, there are entire frameworks to help clinicians provide culturally responsive therapy. Yet few frameworks are assessment focused, and it is rare to find literature on culturally responsive trauma-informed assessment with youth. It is therefore our intention in this chapter to address this gap. We begin by discussing barriers that can result when sociocultural factors are not given sufficient weight during the trauma-informed assessment process.

IDENTIFYING AND ADDRESSING INTENTIONAL AND UNINTENTIONAL BARRIERS

Perhaps the biggest challenge to conducting an effective trauma-informed assessment is the clinician's ability to collect complete and accurate information from the youth and family. Clinicians' sensitivity to sociocultural variables plays a key role in their success in eliciting information from children and families. When clinicians do not take sociocultural variables into consideration, they may encounter a variety of challenges in their attempt to engage and collect information from youth and families during the trauma-informed assessment process. These barriers can be conceptualized as intentional or unintentional.

Addressing Intentional Barriers

Intentional barriers involve a lack of willingness on the part of the youth or family to share information with the clinician. This type of barrier is related to the clinician's ability to help the youth and family feel comfortable and safe during the assessment process, as highlighted in Chapter 2. This chapter builds on Chapter 2 by describing how safety, trust, and rapport may be strongly dependent on the clinician's ability to sensitively make adaptations or modifications to the assessment process in a way that is respectful of and responsive to the child's age, development, and ability as well as a range of sociocultural factors. Likewise, it is important to recognize that the cultural identity and preferences of a youth may differ from those of their parents or caregivers (American Psychological Association, Task Force on Immigration, 2013). For immigrants, this difference is often a product of generational differences in acculturation to the dominant culture (American Psychiatric Association, 2013). When a clinician is not able to create a safe environment for and trusting relationships with children and families, the trauma-informed assessment process may be compromised.

Communication Styles and Patterns

Establishing effective communication is critical to the assessment process. The communication styles and patterns of children and families are influenced by their cultural values, beliefs, and norms. The trauma-informed assessment process described in this book is culturally influenced by a Western mental health perspective. For example, mental health assessments in the United States tend to include a long series of questions to which the client is expected to respond in a clear, concise, and articulate manner (Hays, 2008). During the assessment process, youth and caregivers may be told that they can skip or come back to questions later, but they are also often encouraged to honestly answer as many questions as possible, and they are directly or indirectly dissuaded from providing what the clinician may perceive as "unnecessary" detail.

This approach to gathering personal information from youth and families can feel disorienting and disrespectful to those who come from cultures in which people prefer and are accustomed to sharing personal information in a story-based or narrative way. Thus, it is important that clinicians consider cultural variations in communication patterns and recognize when it may be beneficial to make adjustments to the way they request and receive information—for example, by allowing clients to provide context that might not be critical, by beginning with the client's story and only later asking direct questions to fill in the gaps, or by allowing more time than normal for completing the assessment (Hays, 2008). When differences in communication styles are not acknowledged and respected, the client may feel disconnected or disrespected and inclined to share less information with the clinician, especially in the context of trauma-informed assessment, when families are expected to discuss a variety of sensitive topics.

Sensitive Topics

Most clinicians understand that the discussion of traumatic events can be emotionally upsetting, but they may be less aware of cultural variability regarding other sensitive topics that may be addressed during the assessment process. For instance, asking youth, or even adults, to talk about their caregivers' struggles is counter to some cultural norms and may be considered off limits within certain cultures; people of other cultures may also be hesitant to talk about their religion or spirituality (Hays, 2008). Clinicians are strongly encouraged to approach each assessment with the general understanding that what seems to be an appropriate or "normal" topic of discussion for the dominant culture may be particularly sensitive for some youth and families.

It may be helpful to ask clients directly whether there are any topics they find uncomfortable or would prefer not to discuss, but clinicians must also remember that it is not the youth's or family's responsibility to educate the clinician about their culture (Hays, 2008). Therefore, we recommend that clinicians make efforts to increase their understanding of potential topics that are considered taboo within the cultures of the youth and families they serve (Hays, 2008).

Shared Understanding of the Assessment Process

Shared understanding will be further discussed as a critical component of trauma-informed assessment in Chapter 6. In this chapter, we introduce the idea that a shared understanding of the assessment process, created through openness and transparency, may be especially important for people from sociocultural backgrounds that may make them feel skeptical about assessment. Some groups of people have good reason to be cautious regarding the intentions of unknown providers, and it is very important that they know exactly what to expect during and after the assessment process and that concerns and questions they have are respected and addressed. For example, immigrants with undocumented status in their host country may be concerned that the information provided as part of an assessment could somehow be accessed by authorities who may seek to deport them (de Arellano & Danielson, 2008; Nader, 2008a). Likewise, racial and ethnic minority clients who commonly experience discrimination may be wary of sharing information for fear of being misunderstood or judged (Chavez-Dueñas et al., 2019; de Arellano & Danielson, 2008).

There are a variety of practical recommendations that can help clinicians build a shared understanding with youth and clients from different sociocultural backgrounds. First, the rights of the youth and family (e.g., whether their participation is optional or required, their ability to skip particular questions) and limits of confidentiality should be discussed up front and revisited occasionally during the assessment process. Providers might offer written documentation to their clients regarding how information provided during the assessment process will (and will not) be shared. Second, it is important to provide youth and families with a clear rationale that helps them understand the purpose of the assessment and how it will be used to personally benefit them. Third, clinicians can educate youth and families about the process and content of the assessment and encourage them to ask and make suggestions for how the process could be adjusted to help them feel more comfortable.

Boundaries, Cultural Values, and Disclosure

Families may also present with cultural values and boundaries that create potential barriers in trauma-informed assessment. For example, some cultures adopt an insular family perspective (e.g., "what happens in the family, stays in the family"), which can prevent them from fully disclosing important information during the assessment process. It is important that clinicians watch for this and recognize that families may hold this perspective for a variety of reasons. This insular family dynamic is a norm within some communities, one that is accepted and understood by other members of the cultural group.

Other families, especially those that are marginalized because of race or socioeconomic status, may fear that bringing outside attention to a traumatic event will result in an undesired intervention (e.g., system involvement) or call attention to another problem (e.g., drug use, poverty, homelessness). Youth may be especially unlikely to disclose abuse for fear of getting care-givers in trouble or because they are afraid it is their fault. In some cultures, the entire family may avoid talking openly about specific types of traumatic events (e.g., sexual abuse) because the topic is considered taboo in their religious or ethnic group and could result in judgment and rejection (Fontes & Plummer, 2010). Families from some cultures believe that traumatic events are karmic, or that they happen for a reason (e.g., because a family member committed a sin), and may therefore hesitate to disclose the event during the assessment process (Fontes & Plummer, 2010).

Clinicians who are not sensitive to these types of culturally mediated communication boundaries may not recognize when clients are choosing to purposefully withhold key pieces of information. If clinicians eventually become aware, it is possible that instead of understanding these boundaries as culturally mediated, they will interpret these behaviors as resistance or purposeful intent to mislead. It is therefore recommended that clinicians strive to learn as much as possible about the cultures of the families they serve. Understanding the family's perception of mental health, trauma, and openness about discussing these topics will be beneficial. Providers might also try to educate youth and families about the prevalence of trauma, attempting to normalize their experience. They might also help youth and families understand how trauma is perceived in Western mental health (e.g., never placing blame on the victim).

Acknowledging that some families and cultures consider certain topics off limits or difficult to discuss may create an opportunity for the family to acknowledge their hesitance. It is also helpful to reassure youth and families that they have the right to choose how much and what type of information they share, while helping them simultaneously understand that the clinician's ability to reach helpful conclusions through the assessment is impacted by the amount and accuracy of information provided. Finally, clinicians can suggest that a community leader or cultural broker become involved in the assessment process; a *cultural broker* is someone from the family's cultural group who can help the family understand the importance of speaking openly about trauma and help the clinician know how to best navigate and respect important cultural boundaries.

Addressing Unintentional Barriers

Sometimes unintentional barriers cause breakdowns in communication during the assessment process, even when the clinician has been successful in creating a safe environment and setting the family at ease. These tend to occur when clients try but are not fully able to express themselves in a way that seems relevant or is comprehensible to the clinician. Examples and practical recommendations for addressing unintentional barriers are introduced here, and some are revisited in more detail in the Populations Deserving Special Consideration section below.

Overcoming Language Barriers

A variety of language-related barriers can prevent clinicians from collecting complete and accurate information unless appropriate accommodations are made. Assessment tools should be provided to the youth and family in their preferred language whenever possible. Immigrants who do not speak English as their first language, for example, often benefit from the assistance of a trained professional interpreter. As a rule, youth should not act as interpreters for their caregivers during the trauma-informed assessment process. Interpreters who participate in trauma-informed assessment must be comfortable with and able to navigate the variety of sensitive topics that are likely to be discussed; whenever possible, clinicians should meet with interpreters before and after the assessment to make sure the interpreters understand their role and are comfortable and willing to translate sensitive trauma-related topics (see Hays, 2008, and Miller et al., 2019, for more information on use of interpreters).

Unintentional communication difficulties can also result when the clinician conducting the assessment is unfamiliar with the dialect of youth and families who speak English as a first language; this difficulty can result from regional (e.g., urban vs. rural), race, ethnicity, or class differences. It is also important for clinicians to realize that the youth and family may have equal difficulty understanding the clinician's language. To minimize this possibility, it is recommended that clinicians avoid the use of psychological jargon and academic terms, instead talking about the assessment process and presenting questions in lay language, and periodically check in with the family regarding their understanding. When the clinician struggles to understand the dialect or vocabulary used by the youth and family, it is appropriate to acknowledge this during the assessment, but this must be done respectfully and sensitively, without judgment. The clinician can also ask families for concrete examples and attempt to repeat back what they understood to ensure it is what the family intended to express.

In addition, the way individuals experience and verbally describe trauma-related symptoms varies from culture to culture. When clinicians fail to recognize this variation, it can become an unintentional barrier in the trauma-informed assessment process. Whereas some authors have described posttraumatic stress as an international phenomenon, others have emphasized cultural differences in the expression of posttraumatic symptoms (e.g., people of Asian and Hispanic origin may express a broader range of somatic responses; de Arellano & Danielson, 2008; Osterman & de Jong, 2007). The labels used in the United States to describe trauma-related symptomatology may be confusing or inconsistent with the way people of other cultures think about or describe posttraumatic symptoms (e.g., "hypervigilance" vs. "nervous attack," "flashback" vs. a visit from the spirit of a dead relative; Nader, 2008a). Even broader terms, including "mental health" and "trauma," have culturally mediated differences in definitions and may not have direct translations in some languages because these concepts are so far outside the cultural norms. Clinicians need to keep such differences in labels and definitions in mind and should openly address them during the assessment process, especially when professional translators are involved.

Even within the United States, there are differences in what is understood as "trauma" or "traumatic." Youth growing up in violent communities, for example, may become so accustomed to their exposure that they fail to register it as something potentially traumatic, instead conceptualizing it as a part of their normal, everyday experience (Habib & Labruna, 2011). Speaking broadly with youth and families about their experience of trauma may be beneficial in that it allows for the disclosure of culturally mediated traumatic events that are absent from most assessment measures of trauma exposure. However, because the word "trauma" has become a part of the common social lexicon, asking clients about their exposure to "trauma" may result in the disclosure of any upsetting situation. Therefore, it is always important for clinicians to use objective and descriptive language to ask about specific types of events and to provide examples of experiences that may be viewed as potentially traumatic in the mainstream culture but not necessarily by all people.

Although many of the best assessment measures are available in multiple languages, research rarely provides examples of tools that have gone through the process of becoming culturally relevant with regard to the way items are written and the ways they may be understood by individuals across cultural groups. One exception is the international adaptation of the Adverse Childhood Experiences International Questionnaire (World Health Organization, 2017) and the attempts that were made to ensure that the items are appropriate and understood by members of various communities across the world (e.g., M. Quinn et al., 2018). Readers are encouraged to search the literature for tools that have been culturally adapted for the communities they serve; this research is newly emerging and will likely continue to grow.

Gathering Information From a Variety of Informants

The importance of multiple informants is highlighted in Chapters 3 and 5. Here we discuss how clinicians may miss out on critical information if they fail to include other key adults (e.g., family members who still live in the country of origin, nonkin relatives, healers, religious leaders, respected members of the community who know the youth and family well) who are not traditional informants or reporters in the trauma-informed assessment process (de Arellano & Danielson, 2008; Falicov, 2007). Another unintentional misstep can occur when clinicians fail to observe or respect unfamiliar hierarchical structures that exist within cultures and thereby miss critical pieces of information because they asked the wrong person the wrong type of questions (Hays, 2008).

Once again, avoiding these pitfalls requires that clinicians educate themselves about the cultures of the families they serve. They also need to be willing to think outside the box as they structure the assessment process by being willing to gather information from important adults in the youth's life who may not live in the country using online or telephonic methods (Falicov, 2007). It is probably also a good idea to ask and take recommendations from the youth and family regarding whom they think the clinician needs to talk to as part of the assessment.

Assessing for a Broad Range of Traumatic Events

Assessing for trauma and loss history when working with youth and families from diverse backgrounds presents its own challenges. For example, clinicians who rely entirely on commonly used trauma-informed assessment tools may fail to collect information on the full range of the child's traumatic experiences because the tools were not validated for youth from other countries or because the tools do not list events that are more common in specific parts of the world than in the United States (e.g., kidnapping, torture, human trafficking). Likewise, most assessment tools fail to capture systemic and cumulative traumas such as racism and day-to-day microaggressions.

When they lack culturally sensitive tools, well-intentioned clinicians may unintentionally overlook the importance of assessing for non–life-threatening traumatic experiences that are mediated by cultural values (e.g., an immigrant experiences trauma symptoms as a result of being shamed by their community). For these reasons, it is important that clinicians use well-supported, comprehensive trauma exposure tools and supplement them with tools designed to assess for trauma symptoms related to racism, microaggressions, discrimination, and other forms of systemic trauma (e.g., Williams et al., 2018).

It is also critical that clinicians incorporate questions about traumatic events into their clinical interview. It is unreasonable to think that clinicians can ask about every possible potentially traumatic event; therefore, it is more effective if clinicians encourage youth and families to bring up situations they recall as being extremely stressful or traumatic, even at the risk of families offering information about negative but not necessarily traumatic events. When families respond to this question, clinicians need to be cautious not to assume the event is nontraumatic because it is inconsistent with the exposure criterion (Criterion A) of the posttraumatic stress disorder (PTSD) diagnosis in the *Diagnostic and Statistical Manual of Mental Disorders* (fifth ed. [*DSM-5*]; American Psychiatric Association, 2013), which was developed on the basis of dominant cultures within the Western world. Indeed, the PTSD exposure criterion has evolved over time, and research has demonstrated that some stressful events are significantly predictive of PTSD symptom development even though they do not meet Criterion A in *DSM-5* (Larsen & Berenbaum, 2017).

Another potential barrier occurs when clinicians from the United States work with immigrants or ethnic minority U.S. citizens without having basic knowledge of important historical events that resulted in a shared traumatic experience at the community or societal level (e.g., Rwandan genocide of 1994; kidnapping of 43 Mexican college students in 2014; 2015 chemical explosion in Tianjin, China; Hays, 2008). Clinicians can overcome this barrier by educating themselves about culturally specific historical traumatic events using the academic literature and the Internet.

POPULATIONS DESERVING SPECIAL CONSIDERATION

This section offers considerations and recommendations for potential adjustments to the trauma-informed assessment process based on specific aspects of a client's sociocultural identity. The information is organized in discrete sections, but it is not intended to communicate that children and their families will fit neatly into any one category. Indeed, many individuals easily identify with two or more aspects of identity identified in this chapter, and clinicians must always strive to honor the concept of intersectionality as they learn about and make efforts to be culturally responsive to the clients they serve. Furthermore, it is important to recognize that there is a great deal of diversity within each of the population groups described here and that the recommendations offered will be relevant to varying degrees depending on the individual life experiences and personal preferences of children and their families.

Young Children and Adolescents

Age and developmental stage are important considerations when conducting trauma-informed assessment with children and adolescents. This is true because of age-related differences in the expression of trauma symptoms, as well as the varying ability and willingness to identify and report on symptoms during the assessment process. This section includes recommendations for working with young children and adolescents.

Young Children

Age and developmental stage must be taken into consideration when engaging in trauma-informed assessment, especially when working with very young children. Up to 64% of children aged 2 to 4 years have been exposed to potentially traumatic events (Grasso et al., 2013), and trauma exposure in early childhood is now recognized as creating a "negative cascade effect" on later development and psychological well-being (Enlow et al., 2013). Conducting trauma-informed assessments and accurately diagnosing trauma reactions in young children is therefore incredibly important but can be a time-consuming and complex process (Scheeringa, 2014). Coates and Gaensbauer (2009) identified three specific barriers to effectively assessing for trauma in young children: (a) the child's limited capacity to comprehend and accurately recount the timing of events; (b) the likelihood that the child's development has been derailed as a result of their exposure to trauma, making it difficult to identify whether presenting difficulties are resulting from developmental concerns, trauma, or both; and (c) the relationship between the child and caregiver, which is critical because caregivers are responsible for keeping children safe but some may have been part of the trauma experience.

Accurately identifying PTSD and other trauma responses is a critical piece of the trauma-informed assessment process and, as noted in Chapter 3, is informed by information collected from both the child and the caregiver. However, there is little evidence that children under age 7 can accurately verbalize their own trauma-related symptoms (Scheeringa, 2014). Likewise, symptoms of PTSD in young children are often relational and developmental in nature (e.g., insecure attachment with caregivers, difficulty being soothed; Coates & Gaensbauer, 2009), and the expression of trauma symptoms can change as children develop (Scheeringa, 2014). Both of these issues make accurate diagnosis more challenging, especially for clinicians who do not specialize in working with young children.

Even with slightly older children, accurate reporting of trauma symptoms is strongly reliant on the clinician's ability to engage them and their caregivers with helpful probes for each of the 17 symptoms listed in the PTSD diagnosis in *DSM-5* (American Psychiatric Association, 2013), as well as the caregiver's ability to perceive and accurately report on the subset of symptoms that are internalizing in nature and therefore difficult to observe (Scheeringa, 2014). Furthermore, as highlighted in Chapter 5, there is a lack of consensus regarding which trauma-informed assessment tools are considered the gold standard, especially for young children (Choi & Graham-Bermann, 2018). Finally, many of the existing tools ask respondents to limit their responses about trauma symptoms to those that are related to their "single worst traumatic event," despite the reality that many children experience more than one traumatic event and may have a different pattern of symptoms related to each (Scheeringa, 2014).

To address these challenges, it is recommended that every trauma-informed assessment of a young child incorporate

> a detailed, sequential history of every aspect of the child's traumatic experience, including not only the traumatic event itself but all of the events surrounding the trauma that might influence the internal meanings that the trauma has for that particular child. (Coates & Gaensbauer, 2009, p. 618)

Because of the increased possibility that trauma exposure will disrupt development in early childhood, clinicians are recommended to ask caregivers to report all changes they observed in their child following the traumatic event, even if these symptoms are not classic symptoms of PTSD (Coates & Gaensbauer, 2009). Clinicians are also strongly encouraged to educate families about the range of trauma symptoms they are assessing early in the process (Coates & Gaensbauer, 2009) and to provide age-appropriate examples (Scheeringa, 2014). In addition, it is helpful to ensure that caregivers' endorsement of symptoms is valid by asking them for specific examples (Scheeringa, 2014). Given difficulties with diagnosis, it is recommended that clinicians adhere to the American Academy of Child and Adolescent Psychiatry (2010) policy that all children who are negatively impacted by traumatic stress, regardless of diagnostic status, be provided with evidence-based, trauma-informed interventions.

Adolescents

Conducting trauma-informed assessments with adolescents may also present challenges for clinicians. Adolescents are exposed to traumatic events at higher rates than younger children, likely because of both the passage of time and the achievement of developmental tasks (e.g., separation, individuation) that result in less adult supervision. Adolescents also experience a propensity for risk taking paired with a sense of invulnerability and a still underdeveloped ability to accurately assess and manage dangerous situations (Habib & Labruna, 2011).

Although adolescents have more capacity than young children to identify and verbalize trauma symptoms, they may be more likely to purposefully minimize their reporting of trauma exposure and symptoms. There are multiple contributing factors, including a strong desire to fit in and fear of being judged as different by peers, as well as a desire to avoid self-incrimination by disclosing activities that could be perceived by adults as dangerous or inappropriate and potentially lead to undesired sanctions (e.g., earlier curfew; Habib & Labruna, 2011). This tendency to minimize their reporting can be magnified by a sense of mistrust of unknown adults, especially for youth exposed to racial trauma or those living with ongoing exposure to interpersonal violence (Habib & Labruna, 2011).

Adolescents may also unintentionally minimize trauma symptoms by misinterpreting or even reconceptualizing these symptoms as personality traits. For instance, youth may view symptoms such as the tendency for verbally aggressive outbursts as expressions of strength, especially those who fear that trauma-related symptoms could be perceived as a sign of weakness, perhaps making them a target for additional victimization. Despite their tendency toward minimization, research has suggested that adolescents are a better source of trauma-related information than their caregivers (Habib & Labruna, 2011).

For these reasons, Habib and Labruna (2011) suggested that clinicians working with older youth consciously take several steps to maximize the possibility of collecting complete and accurate information. Some of these guidelines were offered in Chapter 3 as broader recommendations for conducting a comprehensive trauma-informed assessment. Habib and Labruna highlighted the following steps and their relevance to working with adolescents in particular:

- Talk with the youth about the widespread pervasiveness of trauma exposure in an attempt to normalize the youth's experience.

- Use carefully worded, concrete, and objective questions to assess trauma exposure and symptoms while valuing the youth's subjective experience of the event.

- Assess for a range of trauma symptoms, including those that fall outside the diagnostic criteria for PTSD.

- Allow the youth to set limits with regard to the amount of detail they want to provide regarding their trauma exposure.

Habib and Labruna also emphasized the need to readminister trauma assessments over time, including throughout the course of treatment, because adolescents may become more comfortable speaking openly about trauma as they become more aware of and attuned to their own symptoms, less fearful of being judged, and more trusting of the adults administering the assessment.

Finally, the topic of confidentiality is important and may be particularly complex when working with adolescents. In the United States, state law varies regarding the age at which a child can provide consent (vs. assent) for assessment and other psychological services. Until youth are considered legally responsible in this regard, providers may need to share what would otherwise be confidential information from youth with caregivers. Setting clear expectations and boundaries at the start of the assessment process regarding the limits of confidentiality, specifically in relation to caregivers, is essential. For example, clinicians must help adolescents understand what will happen if they choose to disclose information during the trauma-informed assessment process that they do not want their caregivers to be aware of. Clinicians need to also be clear in explaining to both youth and caregivers the types of information they would be required to share with child protective services (e.g., abuse, neglect) or other authorities (e.g., child trafficking, sexual exploitation).

These recommendations for assessment with adolescents are among the most important for professionals conducting trauma-informed assessment. Readers are strongly encouraged to refer to the sources cited for additional recommendations, details, and examples.

Youth With Intellectual or Developmental Disabilities

Children who have intellectual disabilities or developmental disorders (ID/DD) are exposed to a wider range of traumatic events more frequently and are at greater risk of developing PTSD than typically developing youth (Hatton & Emerson, 2004; Mevissen et al., 2016; National Child Traumatic Stress Network [NCTSN], 2004). Traumatic events in the lives of children with ID/DD often go undetected and unreported; when they are reported, authorities rarely investigate crimes against these youth (NCTSN, 2004). In combination, these facts point to the important role of mental health clinicians who engage in trauma-informed assessment with youth who have ID/DD, but there are many inherent challenges that must be kept in mind.

Deciding whether and to what degree to engage children who have ID/DD in the trauma-informed assessment process can be challenging. Although it may be possible to actively involve youth who have relatively minor impairments, it may be impossible to gather information directly from children with more severe deficits, especially those who have language comprehension or expression disabilities. Likewise, there is a relative lack of trauma-focused assessment tools developed for or validated with this population (Wigham et al., 2011; see Chapter 5 for more details on developmental considerations). To address these challenges, it is recommended that clinicians engage with a wide range of caregivers and adults (e.g., parents, other family members, schoolteachers, nurses) as reporters during the assessment process (NCTSN, 2004).

Clinicians who conduct trauma-informed assessment with youth who have ID/DD can become aware of common traits and make accommodations during the assessment process. For example, people with ID/DD tend to think concretely and are highly compliant with authority figures (NCTSN, 2004). They may frequently say "yes" or nod in response to questions they do not fully understand; it is therefore advantageous for providers to speak slowly, clearly, and concretely and to use repetition in creative ways during the trauma-informed assessment process (Dunn, 2018; NCTSN, 2004).

An additional challenge is the lack of clinicians who have expertise in both ID/DD and trauma (Mooney, 2015) and the fact that many youth with ID/DD who are impacted by trauma have difficulty accessing appropriate services (NCTSN, 2004). Although assessing and diagnosing ID/DD fall outside the scope of trauma-informed assessment, it is important that clinicians strive to tease apart ID/DD from delays tied to trauma exposure, which can be difficult, especially for clinicians who lack training in both of these areas (Mooney, 2015). It is recommended that clinicians who conduct trauma-informed assessments address this challenge by fully collaborating with other providers throughout the process (Mooney, 2015). For instance, if a youth presents for a trauma-informed assessment with a diagnosis of ID or DD, it would be good practice for the assessing clinician to reach out to the provider who made the diagnosis to better understand their conceptualization of the child's symptoms. Likewise, it may be important for clinicians to refer families to providers who can conduct an assessment for ID/DD if the trauma-informed assessment suggests delays in these areas. It is critical that providers work together to coordinate their findings and to provide complementary, rather than contradictory, findings and recommendations to youth and families. Readers are encouraged to review the sources referenced in this section, which offer additional details and recommendations.

System-Involved Youth and Families

Almost 700,000 youth were served by the foster care system in 2017 (Children's Bureau, 2018), and in 2014 juvenile courts handled almost 975,000 delinquency cases (Office of Juvenile Justice and Delinquency Prevention, 2018). National statistics on rates of multisystem-involved youth are not available, but research has suggested that one third of youth in the child welfare system may cross over and become juvenile justice involved; rates of child welfare involvement for juvenile justice–involved youth have been as high as 45% (Baglivio et al., 2016). Youth in either or both systems have high rates of trauma exposure (Abram et al., 2004; Kisiel, Fehrenbach, et al., 2009). It is therefore critical that a youth's past or current history of system involvement be taken into consideration during the trauma-informed assessment process.

Several specific recommendations can be made in this regard. First, it is important to screen for *system-induced trauma*, which refers specifically to traumatic experiences and responses that are tied to the youth's system involvement (Goldsmith et al., 2014). These experiences can include separation from siblings and caregivers; failed placements or adoption; frequent moves; discrimination; emotional, physical, or sexual abuse by staff or caregivers; and solitary confinement or other harsh punishments.

Second, it is important for clinicians to remember that youth and families do not enter the child welfare and juvenile justice systems by choice; rather, they are placed in these systems as a result of a determination that the youth or caregiver has done something wrong or illegal. Therefore, engaging system-involved youth and families in the trauma-informed assessment process is different from and potentially more challenging than working with youth and families who independently seek assessment or those who are referred by another provider (NCTSN, 2017).

Growing numbers of system-involved youth are likely to participate in trauma screening and assessment as a required part of their system involvement (Lang et al., 2017). They may be expected by the system to comply and may feel they have no choice but to participate in the assessment process. Likewise, system-involved youth and families may be closely monitored with regard to their compliance, and there may be times when failure to follow through with the assessment or comply with service recommendations results in additional sanctions, especially for youth on probation who are required to receive specific types of mental health interventions (Rosado & Shah, 2007). Literature in this area is scarce, but feeling forced to participate in trauma-informed assessment likely decreases the possibility that youth will openly share information with the provider, either as an attempt to exert some power and control in the situation or because they do not trust the system. System-involved youth or families may also be motivated to minimize their trauma histories or other areas of need to present themselves in a positive light in an effort to more quickly transition out of the system in which they are involved.

Clinicians working with system-involved youth and families can attempt to overcome these barriers in a variety of ways. Determining whether participation in the assessment is optional or required and discussing this with the youth and family is an important first step. Clinicians can also clearly explain the reason for the assessment and describe who will share the assessment findings, with whom, and how. Clinicians can also work closely with other providers in the system to understand and be able to educate the youth and family with regard to the potential impact of assessment findings on their system involvement (Rosado & Shah, 2007). For example, it is important that youth and families know whether findings from the trauma-informed assessment could be used to inform adjudication decisions. As noted in Chapter 3, it may be especially important that clinicians assess youth and family strengths and protective factors in the trauma-informed assessment process with system-involved youth and consider these when developing recommendations (Summersett Williams et al., 2019).

It is also critical that clinicians working with system-involved youth "translate" their trauma-informed assessment findings for the family and the broader system in a way that helps youth, family members, and providers understand the link between the child's trauma history and problematic behaviors (Rozzell, 2013). This translation process is described in more detail in Chapter 6. These efforts on the part of the clinician may help establish trust and rapport with the youth and family. Likewise, systems and providers who understand the causes of a youth's behavior from a trauma perspective and who value a youth's strengths and potential for growth may demonstrate more compassion and leniency in their interactions with system-involved youth and families (Rozzell, 2013).

LGBTQ and Other Sexual and Gender Minority Youth

Children and youth who identify as LGBTQ and other sexual and gender minority youth are deserving of special attention in this chapter for several reasons. First, sexual and gender nonconforming youth have higher rates of exposure to a wide array of interpersonal traumas during their lifetimes, and these victimization experiences frequently occur in response to their perceived or actual gender identity or sexual orientation (McCormick et al., 2018; Mooney, 2017). Second, sexual and gender minority youth and adults are at greater risk of developing PTSD in their lifetime than their heterosexual and cisgender peers (Roberts et al., 2012). Third, LGBTQ youth commonly experience overt (e.g., bullying) as well as covert (e.g., microinsults) forms of discrimination and harassment, which may negatively impact their physical, mental, and emotional health and well-being (Kosciw et al., 2018; Nadal et al., 2016). Fourth, the literature points to high rates of risk behaviors (e.g., substance use, unprotected sex, suicidality) in

LGBTQ youth; when viewed through a trauma-informed lens, these likely are efforts to cope with trauma and other mental health symptoms (McCormick et al., 2018). Finally, and fortunately, research also highlights the power of protective factors, such as acceptance by family and community supports, to facilitate well-being, including positive self-identity and self-esteem (Mooney, 2017).

Taking steps to create a sense of safety for all families is a critical component of trauma-informed assessment. For the reasons outlined above, it may be especially important for LGBTQ youth and their families, who are likely keenly aware of both subtle and overt behavior and messaging when interacting with a new provider. Practitioners engaging in trauma-informed assessment must therefore be knowledgeable about the realities encountered by youth and families in the LGBTQ community; they must also take steps to demonstrate for these youth and families that they are accepting and safe.

One way to show that a provider and agency are safe is by making adaptations to the physical environment that let youth and families know that the space is accepting of all people. Like all individuals, members of the LGBTQ community have many aspects of identity. Therefore, incorporating images (e.g., depicting an array of families and romantic relationships) and messaging (e.g., Safe Zone signs on walls or doors, stickers on employee badges, flags or other decorations with specific cultural significance) that reflect and honor a diversity of sexual orientations, gender identities, races, ethnicities, and religions is a small but important adaptation that can be made (Mooney, 2017).

Clinicians can also make changes to their agency's demographic forms and questionnaires, creating spaces for birth names as well as preferred names and pronouns for all family members, and can commit to using preferred pronouns and names throughout the assessment process. In addition to assessing for a full range of traumatic experiences, it is critical that clinicians sensitively inquire about other harmful or discriminatory experiences that youth and family members may have experienced or be experiencing across multiple settings (e.g., home, school, community).

For LGBTQ youth who are open with the clinician about having a minority sexual orientation or gender identity, it is important to assess the degree to which they feel that their sexual or gender identity is accepted by all members of their family and supported by friends, family, and the broader community; these have been identified as important protective factors for LGBTQ youth (D'Augelli, 2003; Ryan et al., 2010; Simons et al., 2013). Clinicians can also incorporate a self-report measure of discrimination or microaggression, while being mindful that the psychometric properties vary and that some of these tools were designed for research rather than clinical purposes (for a review of these tools, see Fisher et al., 2019). Because LGBTQ youth are at increased risk of an array of negative outcomes and risk behaviors, including running away, homelessness, prostitution, sex trafficking, and suicide, it is critical that providers ask about these issues sensitively and in a variety of ways (e.g., standardized tools, clinical interviews) over time to maximize the possibility of disclosure during the trauma-informed assessment process.

In sum, clinicians can increase safety for youth and families by becoming knowledgeable about issues that may be of particular importance for individuals who identify as LGBTQ. Mooney (2017) suggested that this knowledge can be obtained by seeking out literature and practice guides developed by professional organizations, such as American Psychological Association's "Guidelines for Psychological Practice With Lesbian, Gay, and Bisexual Clients" (American Psychological Association, 2012) and "Guidelines for Psychological Practices With Transgender and Gender Nonconforming People" (American Psychological Association, 2015a). The NCTSN has a wide range of resources about trauma and LGBTQ youth, including webinars such as *Developing Clinical Competence in Working With LGBTQ Youth and Families* (NCTSN, 2014) and *Empowering Therapists to Work With LGBTQ Youth and Families* (NCTSN, 2013; see Appendix A for information on how to access these and additional NCTSN resources).

It is also important that clinicians continuously work to develop awareness of their own biases and expectations regarding LGBTQ populations and that they not make assumptions about the experiences a youth "must be" having. Rather, they should maintain an open mind, be informed about issues that sometimes or often come up for LGBTQ youth (e.g., difficulty related to coming out, school bullying, rejection, humiliation or harm inflicted by homophobic adults), and in the end trust the report of the child and family, even when their experiences appear to differ from those reported in the literature.

People of Color and Indigenous People

Two important concepts—historical trauma and racial trauma—impact POC and Indigenous people. These are key concepts that unfortunately are not yet consistently incorporated into mainstream research or practice, including trauma-informed assessment processes, even by professionals who specialize in the area of trauma. A variety of terms have been used to explain the psychological impact of racism and historical injustices on POC and Indigenous people. An explanation of the origin of these terms and a full review of this literature are beyond the scope of this chapter (see the special issue of *American Psychologist* on racial trauma [Comas-Díaz, Hall, Neville, & Kazak, 2019] for a summary of the recent literature). Definitions and key findings from the current literature are highlighted here to provide readers with a basic orientation and to highlight the importance of considering these types of trauma when conducting trauma-informed assessment with POC and Indigenous people.

Historical trauma refers to the intergenerational impact of "cumulative psychological wounds that result from historical traumatic experiences, such as colonization, genocide, slavery, dislocation, and other related trauma" (Comas-Díaz, Hall, & Neville, 2019, p. 2). The concept of historical trauma derives from research with Indigenous communities, which demonstrates that current generations can experience extreme stress related to the significant harm and trauma experienced by previous generations (e.g., genocide as part of colonization). Studies have demonstrated that people impacted by historical trauma have elevated symptoms of posttraumatic stress and greater vulnerability to PTSD (Mohatt et al., 2014) and that thoughts about the historical traumatic event result in distress that is distinct from that caused by traumatic events they directly experienced (e.g., child abuse; Walls & Whitbeck, 2011).

Racial trauma, which is distinct from historical trauma, refers to the impact of current, day-to-day psychological wounds that occur as a result of repeated exposure to "direct and/or vicarious" and "real or perceived experience of racial discrimination" (Comas-Díaz, Hall, & Neville, 2019, pp. 1–2; see also Chavez-Dueñas et al., 2019). It is not uncommon for people who are impacted by historical trauma to also experience racial trauma, and the impact is likely cumulative. The impact of racial trauma can also reach beyond the individual, affecting entire communities of color (Santiago-Rivera et al., 2016). Research has shown that race-based trauma exposure results in a range of traumatic stress symptoms (e.g., Carter et al., 2020), but only one research study to date has examined the relationship between racial and ethnic discrimination and the diagnosis of PTSD (Sibrava et al., 2019); findings indicated that the frequency of discrimination significantly predicted PTSD diagnosis. Additionally, Sibrava et al. (2019) replicated findings showing that the clinical course of PTSD in African American and Latinx people was poor, even for participants with high rates of treatment utilization.

Youth of color and those with Indigenous heritage make up a substantial proportion of children in the United States, and they are disproportionately overrepresented in the child welfare and juvenile justice systems. It is therefore likely that most clinicians who engage in trauma-informed assessment have done this work with racial and ethnic minority youth and families. There are a variety of potential challenges related to engaging youth of color and those with Indigenous heritage in the assessment process.

Asking youth to open up about their exposure to traumatic events may be challenging, especially for youth of color who, compared with their White peers, may have more difficulty trusting and feeling safe with mental health clinicians or providers in other service systems. This difficulty may be related to their experiences with racism and discrimination at the individual and system level (de Arellano & Danielson, 2008). A relative lack of knowledge regarding historical and racial trauma among mental health providers is an additional barrier, as is the fact that most trauma exposure tools do not incorporate items that assess for racial or historical trauma.

Accurately assessing and understanding the impact of trauma exposure on racial and ethnic minority youth and families can be challenging. It is important to acknowledge that people from some racial and ethnic groups, especially African Americans, are at increased risk of experiencing PTSD and that the course of the diagnosis tends to be more chronic than in White groups (Alegría et al., 2013; Roberts et al., 2011; Sibrava et al., 2019). Although this disparity is not fully understood, recent research demonstrates that racial and ethnic discrimination is predictive of PTSD (but no other anxiety disorder) in both African American and Latinx people (Sibrava et al., 2019). The work in this area has been limited to adult populations, but it is likely that youth have similar predispositions, and this possibility should be kept in mind throughout the assessment process.

A subsequent challenge becomes differentiating reactions to racial trauma from other types of posttraumatic reactions, which requires that a full range of contributing stressors (e.g., PTSD Criterion A stressors, neglect and other attachment-based traumas, exposure to racial discrimination) be taken into consideration during the trauma-informed assessment process. Although there is significant overlap between the symptoms of PTSD and those of racial trauma (Comas-Díaz, Hall, & Neville, 2019), it is important to view them as separate reactions. If for no better reason, this enables the clinician and client to collaboratively choose the most culturally responsive intervention as most empirically supported treatments for children and adults with PTSD have not been developed or adapted to address race-based traumas.

There are several recommendations deserving of consideration. Clinicians who conduct trauma-informed assessments with racial and ethnic minority youth and families may increase the success of the assessment by dedicating extra time and effort to engage youth and their families and help them feel at ease before, during, and after the assessment process. Providers may benefit from talking openly about racial and historical trauma and inviting families to voice any concerns they may have about their participation in the assessment process. As noted earlier in this chapter, it is also important that racial and ethnic minority youth and their families receive information about the assessment process itself, including a clear rationale and what to expect during the assessment and after it is complete. Youth and families should be invited to question, challenge, and correct the clinician's interpretations of the information they share.

As was introduced more broadly in Chapter 2, parsing out the impact of one type of trauma versus another is not a simple task and requires not only a safe space, strong rapport, and a good rationale for the assessment process, but also an ongoing exchange with the client over time to fully appreciate how each trauma has contributed to the development of symptoms and how this information should translate into treatment recommendations. Clinicians who conduct trauma-informed assessment with racial and ethnic minority youth and families need to ensure that they are screening for a variety of potentially traumatic events related to discrimination, racism, and historical trauma. Whenever possible, they should incorporate trauma exposure tools that contain items or are entirely focused on experiences of racial or historical trauma.

Like all individuals, mental health clinicians hold conscious and unconscious biases and may engage in prejudiced behavior toward others (American Psychological Association, Task Force on Immigration, 2013; Merino et al., 2018). In other words, clinicians and researchers from the dominant U.S. culture may be at risk of "assum[ing] the worst about people of minority identities" (Hays, 2008, p. 106). Implicit biases held by mental health providers have been shown to impact the conclusions they draw, including the types of diagnoses, as well as referrals and access to mental health services (Merino et al., 2018). Although not yet well investigated, implicit bias can also negatively impact the trauma-informed assessment process. Current research on mental health more broadly indicates that mental health professionals may hold inaccurate assumptions regarding how POC are impacted by trauma. For example, some providers may assume that youth and families of color are somehow responsible for or deserving of trauma exposure (e.g., victim blaming)—for example, when they believe a youth put themselves in a specific situation leading to the trauma event. These types of implicit biases and others can negatively impact the trauma-informed assessment process and the validity of the conclusions drawn by the clinician (Merino et al., 2018) in a variety of ways, such as by influencing the types of questions asked and the clinician's interpretation of the youth's response. Implicit biases on the part of clinicians can also contribute to inequities in access to mental health services (Merino et al., 2018).

Clinicians who conduct trauma-informed assessments therefore need to actively work to cultivate awareness of their own assumptions about different racial and ethnic groups, engage in frequent consultation regarding these topics with colleagues and supervisors, and pursue relevant professional development opportunities. They must also strive to become aware of shared societal biases (e.g., viewing men of color as particularly dangerous) that may be perpetuated through media and the potential impact these biases have on POC and Indigenous people. It is also critical that clinicians who engage in trauma-informed assessment remember that there is extreme diversity within every racial and ethnic group, and that the people they serve from specific racial or ethnic groups may be more different than alike.

Children Who Are Immigrants and Refugees

Many immigrants and refugees leave their countries of origin to escape ongoing exposure to traumatic events (e.g., crime, interpersonal violence, war, torture), and large numbers of immigrants experience additional trauma during and postmigration to their host country (American Psychological Association, Task Force on Immigration, 2013; Chavez-Dueñas et al., 2019). For example, a mother who was stalked, kidnapped, and raped in her country of origin may be exposed to additional physical and sexual violence on her journey, especially if she is reliant on smugglers or other nonlegal methods of entering the host country. Upon arrival, she may risk additional trauma exposure, including forced separation from her children, ethnic profiling, discrimination, and deportation. A systematic review found that traumatic events occurring before, during, and after migration were risk factors for mental health problems among refugee children (van Os et al., 2016). Many immigrant youth and families also experience the loss of social capital and support networks when they immigrate, which may reduce their resilience when faced with traumatic stressors in the host country (American Psychological Association, Task Force on Immigration, 2013).

One barrier to trauma-informed assessment with immigrant and refugee children is that many commonly used trauma screening and assessment tools do not address traumatic events that are related to the migration experience or, as noted earlier in this chapter, events that are less common in the mainstream U.S. culture than in other parts of the world (American Psychological Association, Task Force on Immigration, 2013). Another barrier is that many trauma assessment tools have not been validated for use with immigrant populations, and tools designed specifically for immigrant and refugee populations are quite limited (American Psychological Association, Task Force on Immigration, 2013; Gadeberg et al., 2017; Gadeberg & Norredam, 2016). Although a small number of trauma-informed assessment tools have been validated for use with one or more refugee populations (Gadeberg et al., 2017), most clinicians still rely on interviews and tools that are not validated for use with refugees (Gadeberg & Norredam, 2016).

Researchers have additionally speculated that tools designed for the mainstream U.S. population underestimate the prevalence of trauma-related symptomatology in refugees. This is problematic because research has clearly pointed to a relationship between the number and types of stressful life events and the occurrence of posttraumatic stress reactions in both accompanied and unaccompanied children (van Os et al., 2016).

Several recommendations more fully described earlier in this chapter are worth briefly repeating here, including

- the potential benefits of identifying and connecting with long-distance family members, including caregivers who still reside in the child's country of origin, and being creative with ways to include them in the assessment process;

- the benefits and challenges of working closely with trauma-informed interpreters; and

- the need to become educated about the cultures of the children and families being served.

Seeking additional information from other sources is another critically important recommendation, especially for clinicians who frequently conduct trauma-informed assessments with refugee and migrant youth.

Although the peer-reviewed literature in this area is still scant, one notable exception is an article by de Arellano and Danielson (2008) that described their INFORMED model, which consists of eight recommendations for modifying trauma assessment of culturally diverse populations:

- Investigate the target population;
- Navigate new ways of delivering assessment services based on study of target population;
- Further assess extended family and other collaterals;
- Organize the background assessment to better accommodate the target population;
- Recognize and broaden the range of traumatic events to be assessed;
- Modify types of trauma-related sequelae assessed;
- Evaluate the effectiveness of the modified assessment; and
- Develop the assessment based on its evaluation. (p. 56)

Most of de Arellano and Danielson's recommendations are consistent with those covered elsewhere in this chapter, but their article provides additional helpful details such as creative ways clinicians can learn about and connect with immigrant populations residing in their town or city.

Over the past decade, nonprofit organizations and federally funded initiatives (e.g., National Child Traumatic Stress Initiative) have produced many helpful resources regarding trauma work with immigrants and refugees. The NCTSN (2019) summarized these written and virtual educational materials in a document titled "Select NCTSN Resources Related to Refugee and Immigrant Trauma," which can be downloaded from the NCTSN website (https://www.nctsn.org). Three of the 34 resources highlighted in this document are focused specifically on assessment in refugee youth, but all contain information that can be beneficial to clinicians who want to know more about the immigrant and refugee populations they assess.

CONCLUSION

It is important that clinicians remember that critical information can be intentionally or unintentionally withheld during the trauma-informed assessment process. This possibility can be minimized when clinicians follow the practical recommendations included in this chapter. First, clinicians need to remember that children and families who participate in trauma-informed assessment vary greatly with regard to their comfort during and expectations about the assessment process. Individuals who have been marginalized and discriminated against by the dominant culture may feel skeptical about the intent of the clinician who conducts the trauma-informed assessment, wary about the components of the assessment process, and fearful about how they will be understood and treated throughout the process.

Second, it is the responsibility of the provider to create a professional environment that is safe and welcoming for all people. Third, clinicians who work with clients from sociocultural backgrounds that are different from their own should approach the assessment process in a curious and humble manner and seek out both continued professional education and less formal opportunities (e.g., peer consultation, supervision) to increase their cross-cultural knowledge and sensitivity.

Fourth, it is important that all clinicians who engage in trauma-informed assessment engage in ongoing work to cultivate self-awareness regarding how their own personal privilege, experiences, beliefs, and biases may impact their work with children and families from other cultural groups.

The ADDRESSING model (Hays, 1996, 2008, 2016) was designed to assist mental health professionals in the examination of their own biases and areas of inexperience by understanding the relevance of nine main cultural influences: **A**ge and generational influences, **D**evelopmental or other **D**isability, **R**eligion and spirituality, **E**thnic and racial identity, **S**ocioeconomic status, **S**exual orientation, **I**ndigenous heritage, **N**ational origin, and **G**ender.

As noted by the American Psychological Association (2017), psychological assessments should be "culturally tailored and ecologically relevant" (p. 56). Therefore, it is recommended that the topics addressed in this chapter be fully incorporated into every graduate training program and clinical internship and that steps be taken to ensure that trainees of color and those from the dominant culture all receive support as they explore these topics with colleagues and clients.

5 SELECTING AND INTEGRATING TRAUMA-INFORMED ASSESSMENT TOOLS FOR CHILDREN AND ADOLESCENTS

A crucial part of the trauma-informed assessment process is the use of tools to assist in the gathering of information, along with the additional assessment techniques identified in Chapter 3. Yet historically, clinicians have been somewhat reticent about incorporating tools into their assessment process, often believing that they could gather the same information without going through the time-consuming process of administering a tool and scoring it in a timely manner (J. R. Cook et al., 2017; Ionita & Fitzpatrick, 2014; Meehl, 1996). J. R. Cook and colleagues (2017) suggested that clinicians were more likely to use unstandardized tools or processes (e.g., informal behavioral observation, unstructured clinical interview) in their practice in general, although this likelihood varied by level of education, training, and professional role; generally, psychologists may be more likely to use standardized tools.

As funders and administrators have begun to emphasize the importance of treatment outcomes and evidence-based assessment practices, it has become critical to incorporate the use of assessment tools that have empirical support into the process. Although several assessment tools and resources

https://doi.org/10.1037/0000233-005
Trauma-Informed Assessment With Children and Adolescents: Strategies to Support Clinicians, by C. Kisiel, T. Fehrenbach, L. Conradi, and L. Weil

are available to clinicians who are committed to integrating trauma-informed assessments into their work, the process of identifying and selecting specific tools can be somewhat overwhelming. Clinicians are encouraged to integrate tools into their practice to ensure that information is gathered from multiple reporters and informants and through use of various assessment techniques. Even if clinicians do not have access to some of the tools that come with a cost, many existing tools are free and can provide helpful information on children's and youths' experiences and symptoms.

CONTEXTUAL FACTORS TO CONSIDER WHEN SELECTING TRAUMA-INFORMED ASSESSMENT TOOLS FOR CHILDREN AND ADOLESCENTS

In addition to the need to determine whether a tool assesses the domains highlighted in Chapter 3, Strand and colleagues (2005) advocated for considering additional contextual factors when selecting a trauma-informed assessment tool for use with children and adolescents. These factors include information on the properties of the tool (e.g., reliability, validity) and the settings or contexts in which it has been used (e.g., clinic or community, ethnically diverse populations) to ensure the tool meets the identified needs of the children and adolescents served in specific settings. Finally, it is useful to consider several practical issues, including the administration time, cost, and format of the tool and whether the tool works in a particular setting (e.g., child report versus provider report; Strand et al., 2005). In the sections that follow we describe the contextual factors that should be considered during the trauma-informed assessment process, including the use of multiple informants and tool formats, factors for consideration across settings, the age and developmental level of the child, and cultural considerations.

Use of Multiple Informants and Tool Formats

As outlined in Chapter 3, gathering information from multiple informants is an essential component of a trauma-informed assessment process. Some tools have been designed to be completed by the child, whereas others have been designed to be completed by the parent or caregiver or the clinician or other provider (Conradi et al., 2011; Kisiel, Conradi, et al., 2014).

Child Self-Report

A child self-report tool can be a helpful way to gather information on the child's experience if the tool is developmentally appropriate and the child can read and comprehend it. Most child self-report tools can be considered for children aged 8 and above, but it is recommended that these tools be used at the therapist's discretion based on their perception of how well the child may be able to share their thoughts in this manner. For some youth, a self-report tool can provide an opportunity to share their experiences within the "privacy" of a pencil-and-paper format, versus verbalizing it aloud. Other youth may prefer to share their experiences aloud or in some other format. A child's self-report can provide the clinician with critical information regarding internalizing symptoms, something that caregivers are less likely to fully understand and be able to report on accurately (Hawkins & Radcliffe, 2006).

Caregiver and Other Provider Report

In most situations, it is critical to gather information from the caregiver and other care providers or from collateral reports in the child's life as part of the assessment process. For young children (aged 0–8) or children with language or other developmental delays, it is essential to gather feedback from caregivers as they are the only individuals who are likely to be able to share the child's history as well as concerning symptoms. Even for older youth, the caregiver perspective can provide critical information on how the youth is functioning and bring to light any discrepancies between the youth's and caregiver's interpretation of behaviors, other responses, and events that have occurred.

It is highly recommended that information also be gathered from additional individuals in the child's life who see the child frequently and have a sense of the potential concerns and challenging behaviors. These individuals may include teachers, caseworkers, and other direct service staff. Gathering assessment data from several reporters provides information from multiple perspectives, which can create a clearer picture of how the youth interacts and copes across various settings. For example, the teacher may share several concerns that are unknown to the caregiver but shed light on how the youth is behaving in school. Pulling together information across all of these perspectives and settings can assist the clinician in establishing a clearer understanding of the youth and their functioning (Conradi et al., 2011).

Making Sense of Discrepant Information

Gathering information from multiple informants provides critical feedback on how the child, caregiver, and family are functioning; these various informants may have different points of view on critical issues. For instance, it is not uncommon for the caregiver's and child's reports of symptoms and functioning to have some discrepancies. The clinician is often charged with the task of identifying treatment goals even when the caregiver and youth disagree about the symptom presentation. When a clinician encounters inconsistent reports, they must draw on other sources of information, such as the clinical interview, observation, and collateral sources, to determine which report most accurately reflects the youth's current functioning.

In general, there tends to be poor agreement between youth and caregiver reports of exposure to traumatic events and related reactions during the period of time around the trauma (Oransky et al., 2013). When a caregiver denies problems that a youth reports, it may be a signal for the clinician to address family and systemic needs. It is important for clinicians to understand that discrepant reports may have many different meanings. For example, the youth may exhibit different observable behaviors in different settings, different observers may have different inherent ability or sensitivity to observe and report different types of behaviors (e.g., internalized vs. externalized) and thus may be more or less reliable reporters of different types of problems, and all observers, including the clinician, may be bringing their own biases to observing, interpreting, and reporting the youth's behaviors. This is where clinical judgment becomes an important part of the process (Kisiel, Conradi, et al., 2014). Although these discrepancies may present some challenges, they also offer an opportunity for engagement and discussion between family members in the context of treatment (Kisiel, Blaustein, et al., 2009).

Factors for Consideration Across Settings

Each trauma-informed assessment will be informed by the setting in which it occurs, as well as by the level of trauma training of the staff engaging in screening or assessment (Kisiel, Conradi, et al., 2014). For instance, assessments in the context of disaster response are likely to involve a targeted, triage-based, safety and services deployment orientation in the short term (Speier, 2006), whereas over the longer term they may take the form of a clinical evaluation with a more in-depth focus on trauma exposure and symptom-based assessment among youth that is typical of an outpatient clinic setting (as described in Chapter 3). School-based trauma-informed assessment may initially focus on manifestations of the trauma response most obviously related to difficulties with school behavior and achievement. However, in order to integrate these findings into a comprehensive picture of a child's overall trauma-related symptoms, clinicians in school-based settings may benefit from training on assessment that uses a wider "trauma lens" (Tishelman et al., 2010).

In pediatric medical settings, a child's unique physical health care needs should be integrated with their mental health care needs, involving collaboration between medical social workers, psychological or psychiatric services, and physicians in the assessment process. In pediatric medical settings as well as other systems, such as child welfare, schools, and juvenile justice, a trauma screening may be administered to identify individuals who may be experiencing the effects of trauma but haven't yet been referred to a mental health provider. In these situations, the screener can assist in identifying children who would benefit from a more comprehensive trauma-informed assessment conducted by a clinician.

Age and Developmental Considerations

Selection of assessment tools and strategies should also be determined by specific age and developmental considerations. Although a large number of trauma-focused tools exist, there is a lack of consensus about which are considered the gold standard, especially for young children (Choi & Graham-Bermann, 2018). Some tools are designed to assess children across a broad developmental spectrum, whereas others are designed to focus on a specific age range. These differences will impact what type of tools are selected, how they are administered, and how they are interpreted within the content of clinical work. Exposure to trauma can have a pervasive impact across areas of development and functioning, and it is important to consider these effects in the context of a child's age and developmental stage. This section highlights some important considerations for young children, school-age children, and adolescents. For a more detailed review of the intersection between trauma and developmental disabilities, see Chapter 4.

The assessment of trauma in young children presents a set of unique challenges and barriers. Because young children are unable to complete assessment tools on their own, their caregiver is most likely to be the respondent for any tools that are completed as part of the assessment. Although there is incongruity and lack of consensus about tools for young children, Coates and Gaensbauer (2009) recommended that clinicians work with the family to complete a semistructured interview for posttraumatic stress disorder (PTSD) and symptoms, tools for complex trauma symptoms, and multiple observational assessments of the child and caregiver to provide information on the child's relationship with the caregiver. Unlike other age groups, for young children there are fewer tools designed specifically to assess trauma exposure, reactions, and traumatic stress responses.

Some commonly used tools include the Diagnostic Infant and Preschool Assessment–PTSD scale (Scheeringa & Haslett, 2010), the Pediatric Emotional Distress Scale (Saylor et al., 1999), the Trauma Symptom Checklist for Young Children (TSCYC; Briere, 2005), and the PTSD in Preschool Aged Children scale (Levendosky et al., 2002).

In school-age children, the process of using assessment tools is somewhat more straightforward. School-age children are more likely than young children to be able to share information on an assessment tool about any trauma they have experienced and any related traumatic stress reactions or symptoms. There are tools that can be completed by children over age 9 if deemed developmentally appropriate. As described previously, it can be helpful to have both the child and the caregiver complete different versions of the same trauma-informed assessment tool. For example, children aged 9 or older may be able to complete the Trauma Symptom Checklist for Children (TSCC; Briere, 1996) on their own while their caregiver completes the TSCYC, a related measure with similar domains. The use of these different, yet related, tools can provide helpful information on the child's and caregiver's differing perspectives. Tools to assess exposure, reactions, and traumatic stress responses in children are highlighted in more detail in the sections that follow and listed in Table 5.1.

Adolescents may have a greater cognitive capacity to share their experiences of trauma and subsequent reactions or symptoms, but they may also be more self-conscious or anxious about disclosing specific events or symptoms during an assessment, especially if they are unsure about whom the information will be shared with. Additionally, adolescents who have been exposed to trauma on a chronic basis may not identify their experiences as traumatic and may normalize both their experiences and any reactions related to the trauma. Many of the tools highlighted in Table 5.1 can be used with adolescents, and some tools were designed specifically for this population, including the Adolescent Dissociative Experiences Scale (Armstrong et al., 1997) and the Youth Self-Report (Achenbach & Rescorla, 2001).

It is also important to remember that the expression of trauma symptoms can change as children develop and that the course of PTSD symptomatology may be more chronic in children than in adults, regardless of whether children meet full diagnostic criteria for PTSD (Scheeringa, 2014). Many of the tools, especially diagnostic instruments, ask respondents to focus on and limit their responses to symptoms that are related to their single worst traumatic event, despite the reality that many children experience more than one traumatic event and may have a different pattern of symptoms related to each (Scheeringa, 2014).

TABLE 5.1. List of Trauma-Informed Assessment Tools for Children and Adolescents

Name of tool	Citation	Number of items	Domains measured	Respondent	Age range	Cost and access	Languages
Acute Stress Checklist for Children (ASC-Kids)	Kassam-Adams, 2006	29	Trauma exposure	Youth	8–17	Free	English, Spanish
Adolescent Dissociative Experiences Scale (A-DES)	Armstrong et al., 1997	29	Trauma reactions	Youth	11–17	Free	English
Child and Adolescent Needs and Strengths (CANS)–Trauma Comprehensive Version	Kisiel et al., 2013	110	Trauma reactions, PTSD reactions, complex trauma	Clinician	0–18	Free	English
Child Behavior Checklist (CBCL)	Achenbach & Rescorla, 2001	120	Broad functioning	Caregiver	6–18	Cost; contact ASEBA	Multiple
Child Dissociative Checklist (CDC)	Putnam et al., 1993	20	Trauma reactions	Caregiver	5–12	Free	English
Child PTSD Symptom Scale (CPSS)	Foa et al., 2001	Part 1: 17, Part 2: 7	Trauma reactions, PTSD reactions	Youth	8–18	Free	English, Korean, Russian, Spanish
Child's Reaction to Traumatic Events Scale-Revised (CRTES-R)	R. T. Jones et al., 2002	23	Trauma reactions	Youth	6–18	Free	English, Spanish
Children's PTSD Inventory (CPTSD-I)	Saigh, 2004	50	Trauma reactions, PTSD reactions	Youth	6–18	Cost involved, contact Harcourt Assessment	English, French, Spanish
Child Sexual Behavior Inventory (CSBI)	Friedrich, 1997	38	Trauma reactions	Caregiver	2–12	Introductory kit available from Psychological Assessment Resources; $230 for 50 booklets	English

(continues)

TABLE 5.1. List of Trauma-Informed Assessment Tools for Children and Adolescents (Continued)

Name of tool	Citation	Number of items	Domains measured	Respondent	Age range	Cost and access	Languages
Clinician-Administered PTSD Scale for *DSM*-5, Child and Adolescent Version (CAPS-CA-5)	Pynoos et al., 2015	30	Trauma reactions, PTSD reactions, diagnostic	Clinician	7-18	Contact National Center for PTSD for pricing and to obtain scale	English
Developmental Trauma Disorder Semi-Structured Interview (DTD-SI)	Ford et al., 2018	15	Trauma reactions, complex trauma	Caregiver	0-18	Free	English
Diagnostic Infant and Preschool Assessment-PTSD scale (DIPA PTSD)	Scheeringa & Haslett, 2010	63	Trauma exposure, trauma reactions, PTSD reactions, diagnostic	Caregiver	0-6	Free	English
Diagnostic Interview for Children and Adolescents Acute Stress Disorder Module (DICA-ASD)	Miller et al., 2004	58	Trauma exposure, trauma reactions, PTSD reactions, diagnostic	Youth	7-18	Free	English
Juvenile Victimization Questionnaire (JVQ)	Hamby et al., 2011	34	Trauma exposure	Youth	8-17	Free, but cite correctly	English
Kauai Recovery Index (KRI)	Hamada et al., 2003	24	Trauma exposure, trauma reactions	Youth	6-15	Free	English
Parent Report of Posttraumatic Stress Symptoms (PROPS)	Greenwald & Rubin, 1999	32	Trauma reactions, PTSD reactions	Caregiver	7-17	$15-$20	Multiple
Pediatric Emotional Distress Scale (PEDS)	Saylor et al., 1999	21	Trauma reactions	Caregiver	2-10	Free	English, Spanish

Instrument	Citation	Items	Content	Informant	Age	Cost	Language
PTSD in Preschool Aged Children (PTSD-PAC)	Levendosky et al., 2002	18	Trauma reactions, PTSD reactions, diagnostic	Caregiver	2-5	Free	English
PTSD Semi-Structured Interview and Observational Record (PTSD-SSI)	Scheeringa & Zeanah, 1994	29	Trauma exposure, trauma reactions, PTSD reactions, diagnostic	Caregiver	0-7	Free	English
Structured Interview for Disorders of Extreme Stress-Adolescent Version (SIDES-A)	Habib et al., 2005	45	PTSD reactions	Youth	12-18	Free	English
Trauma and Attachment Belief Scale (TABS)	Pearlman, 2003	84	Trauma reactions	Self	9-99	$145 intro kit	English
Trauma Symptom Checklist for Children (TSCC)	Briere, 1996	54	Trauma reactions	Youth	8-16	$237 intro kit	English, Spanish
Trauma Symptom Checklist for Young Children (TSCYC)	Briere, 2005	90	Trauma reactions	Caregiver	3-12	$310 intro kit	English, Spanish
Traumatic Events Screening Inventory-Revised (TESI)	Ghosh-Ippen et al., 2002	24	Trauma exposure, trauma reactions	Youth and caregiver versions	6-18	Free	English
UCLA PTSD Reaction Index (PTSD-RI)	Steinberg et al., 2004	48	Trauma exposure, trauma reactions	Youth	6-18	$1.20-$1.30 per instrument	Multiple
Violence Exposure Scale for Children-Revised (VEX-R)	Fox & Leavitt, 1995	25	Trauma exposure	Youth and caregiver versions	4-10	Free	English, Hebrew, Spanish
Youth Self-Report	Achenbach & Rescorla, 2001	112	Broad functioning	Youth	11-18	Cost involved, contact ASEBA	Multiple

Note. ASEBA = Achenbach System of Empirically Based Assessment; *DSM-5* = *Diagnostic and Statistical Manual of Mental Disorders*, fifth ed.; PTSD = posttraumatic stress disorder; UCLA = University of California, Los Angeles. From "Assessing the Effects of Trauma in Children and Adolescents in Practice Settings," by C. Kisiel, L. Conradi, T. Fehrenbach, E. Torgersen, and E. C. Briggs, 2014, *Journal of Child and Adolescent Psychiatric Clinics of North America*, 23(2), pp. 230–231 (https://doi.org/10.1016/j.chc.2013.12.007). Copyright 2014 by Elsevier. Adapted with permission.

Cultural Considerations

Incorporating cultural sensitivity into the trauma-informed assessment process is necessary in order to gather an accurate picture of the child's or youth's functioning within the context of the larger system within which they interact. More specifically, it is important to use assessment tools that are available in the family's primary language. Multiple tools have been translated into several languages, with research conducted on the use of the tool with that specific language. Table 5.1 specifies which tools have been translated into different languages. Moreover, clinicians should consider whether the tool has been used with or has norms applicable to the population served. For a more comprehensive review of how trauma-informed assessment interfaces with sociocultural considerations, see Chapter 4.

KEY QUESTIONS TO CONSIDER WHEN SELECTING TRAUMA-INFORMED ASSESSMENT TOOLS FOR CHILDREN AND ADOLESCENTS

Prior to selecting measures to use for assessment purposes, there are some key questions for clinicians to consider (Kisiel, Conradi, et al., 2014). The choice of assessment tools sometimes depends on the types of events the child has experienced and the initial symptoms. Although the resources and staff capacity at a given agency need always be taken into consideration, it is recommended that normed measures with solid psychometric properties be used whenever possible. These tools are sometimes costly to purchase, and administering them may require specialized training or licensure, but they can also allow for more reliable findings. There are times when the burden associated with specific techniques (e.g., lengthy diagnostic interview schedules) may outweigh the benefits. Finally, it may be that the initial trauma-informed assessment process identifies issues that are more appropriately referred for a specialized assessment (e.g., neuropsychological testing for cognitive processing issues, occupational therapy assessment for motor abnormalities). Table 5.2 highlights key questions for an agency or practitioner to consider when identifying and implementing assessment tools.

OVERVIEW OF TOOLS FOR TRAUMA-INFORMED ASSESSMENT

After committing to implementing a comprehensive trauma-informed assessment process for children and adolescents within a practice or agency, the next step is to identify which tools to incorporate. There is a broad range of

TABLE 5.2. Key Questions to Consider When Implementing Assessment Tools

Domain	Questions
Purpose	What is the purpose of the tool?
	Can we use it to facilitate decision making or inform clinical practice?
Research	What type of research has been conducted on the tool?
	Does it have established reliability and validity and norms?
	Has it been used with diverse (e.g., ethnically and racially) populations?
Language	Is the tool available in the languages used by our clients?
Cost	How can we obtain the measure?
	Are certain qualifications required to order or administer the measure?
	What is our budget?
	What is the cost of the tool?
Administration and scoring	How long does the tool take to administer? Are there specific time constraints in our setting?
	Are there a range of formats we can use (e.g., self-report, caregiver report, provider or clinician report)?
	How is the measure scored? Do we need to work with information technology to create a system that scores and stores the information?
Feedback	Are we able to provide feedback to the clinician and other staff in an efficient, understandable, and timely manner?
	How is the information shared with the clinician? How is that information then shared with the child, caregiver, and family?
Staff education, training, and experience	What staff do we have available to administer the tool?
	What is their level of education and experience?
	How much extra time is involved in completing the measure and then using the information for case and treatment planning purposes?
Measurement of change over time	Does the measure track change over time and allow us to see whether the child or adolescent has improved?

Note. From "Assessing the Effects of Trauma in Children and Adolescents in Practice Settings," by C. Kisiel, L. Conradi, T. Fehrenbach, E. Torgersen, and E. C. Briggs, 2014, *Journal of Child and Adolescent Psychiatric Clinics of North America, 23*(2), pp. 230–231 (https://doi.org/10.1016/j.chc.2013.12.007). Copyright 2014 by Elsevier. Adapted with permission.

tools for trauma-informed assessment, and multiple considerations need to be addressed during the selection process. The sections that follow provide recommendations for clinicians and agencies interested in implementing the use of these tools in their practice.

Previous Reviews of Assessment Tools for Child and Adolescent Trauma

There are multiple reviews within the literature on trauma-informed assessment tools that provide an overview of existing tools and offer important considerations for selecting and implementing these tools in practice. One of the earliest reviews of trauma-informed assessment tools was conducted by Ohan and colleagues (2002), who evaluated their properties as reported in publications from the previous 25 years. Their findings suggested that at that time, the field of tools investigating trauma and its effects in children and adolescents was in its infancy. The authors concluded that trauma-related scales showed promise for research and clinical use in understanding youth responses to trauma. However, their utility for treatment planning and for accountability in practice was generally not as clear.

Soon after, Strand et al. (2005) reviewed 35 tools for trauma-informed assessment, 25 in depth and 10 in brief, that were available in 2005 to researchers and practitioners. The tools were divided into four domains: those that screen for (a) both a history of exposure to traumatic events and symptoms of trauma, (b) only a history of exposure, (c) symptoms of PTSD or dissociation, and (d) multiple trauma-related symptoms (e.g., depression, anger, sexual concerns, PTSD). They summarized information about the type of tool, the purpose of the tool, psychometric properties, and practical issues and provided a brief analysis of clinical utility for each of the 25 tools. This review was the first to highlight that a multitude of measures existed for trauma, whether for a specific trauma or more generally. However, the authors noted that although many tools existed, there were gaps as well, including a lack of tools specified by age group and few measures focused on identifying multiple trauma symptoms outside of PTSD, particularly for adolescents.

In that same year, Briere and Spinazzola (2005) presented one of the earliest frameworks on conducting a structured, psychometrically sound assessment of a child's trauma history and symptoms. In this review, the authors highlighted several tools specifically focused on trauma-informed assessment. This review reflects the beginning of conversations focused more broadly on the use of trauma-informed assessment tools specific to various domains to create a more comprehensive assessment process, the need to organize the information effectively, and the ways findings can be used in practice to drive treatment planning efforts rather than solely to support research studies. In addition, this review offered consideration of tools that measured symptoms outside the basic diagnostic criteria for PTSD, imploring clinicians to consider complex trauma symptomatology.

More recently, Kisiel, Conradi, et al. (2014) presented a model of trauma-informed assessment that highlights specific domains to include in the trauma-informed assessment process across practice settings and identified tools that can be used for these specific domains, including trauma exposure and trauma symptoms. This review also highlighted the importance of assessing the broader changes in functioning that may occur following exposure to one or multiple traumatic events and identified tools that address those changes. The review also emphasized the importance of assessing for child and caregiver strengths in addition to needs. An update and expansion of this review is contained in Chapter 3 of the current text with a focus on key domains.

The next year, Milne and Collin-Vezina (2015) published a tailored review of assessment tools focused specifically on child welfare–involved youth placed in out-of-home care. This review was one of the first to propose a cluster of measures suitable for a standardized trauma-focused assessment procedure specifically aimed at children and youth involved in the child welfare system in order to identify the need for trauma-focused services.

In 2017, Denton and colleagues updated the Strand et al. (2005) review by identifying trauma-informed assessment tools that had been developed or evaluated since the earlier review and determining which were developmentally appropriate for children or adolescents with histories of complex trauma. They identified 35 papers that evaluated 29 measures assessing general functioning and mental health ($n = 11$), PTSD ($n = 7$), and trauma symptomatology outside or in addition to PTSD ($n = 11$). Studies were evaluated in terms of sample quality, trauma or adversity type, and demographic and psychometric data. A distinction was made between measures validated for children (aged 0–12 years) and adolescents (aged 12–18 years). They found that many of the measures were potentially promising but needed further research.

In addition to the reviews of assessment tools, there are multiple resources that serve as a repository of trauma-informed assessment tools that may be helpful for clinicians to review; these are included in Appendix A. The reviews provide helpful information on the wide range of trauma-informed assessment tools available for children of different ages, summarize research on these tools, and describe how they have been applied across domains and settings. It is recommended that clinicians become familiar with these reviews and the available tools so that they can consider which kinds of tools make sense to implement in their trauma-informed assessment process.

Review of Existing Tools for Trauma-Informed Assessment by Domain

In Chapter 3, we reviewed the recommended domains to assess during a comprehensive trauma-informed assessment process. Whereas some of the domains introduced in Chapter 3 may be best explored during a clinical interview (e.g., family history), there are several assessment tools that can assist the clinician in gathering the relevant information across these domains using psychometrically valid and reliable measures. In this section, we provide information on tools that complement many of the domains of assessment introduced in Chapter 3, specifically trauma exposure and loss history, adverse and stressful life experiences, developmental history, trauma responses, family and caregiver trauma history and functioning, and strengths.

Trauma Exposure and Loss History

Multiple screening and assessment tools focus specifically on the child's exposure to traumatic events, including the Acute Stress Checklist for Children (Kassam-Adams, 2006), the Juvenile Victimization Questionnaire (Hamby et al., 2011), the Violence Exposure Scale for Children–Revised (Fox & Leavitt, 1995), and the Traumatic Events Screening Inventory–Revised (Ghosh-Ippen et al., 2002). The types of events that are captured by these tools usually include child abuse and neglect, other forms of interpersonal violence, anthropogenic and natural disasters, community violence and war, and traumatic separation or loss. Other types of trauma that may be assessed include historical trauma, racial trauma, and system-induced trauma.

In some cases, these tools are used by providers in child-serving systems (e.g., child welfare, juvenile justice, schools) to determine whether a child would benefit from a referral for a trauma-informed assessment. In other cases, clinicians may use these tools to assist them in understanding the child's experiences of trauma, which may be far more extensive and complex than the initial reason for the referral for services. These tools vary somewhat in the types of events they include, and some, but not all, have questions regarding trauma responses (described below). Table 5.1 provides information on the most commonly used tools for assessing trauma exposure and loss history in children and adolescents.

Adverse and Stressful Life Experiences

Chapter 3 introduced the Adverse Childhood Experiences (ACE) Study, a landmark study that highlighted the correlation between early adversity and long-term health outcomes (Felitti et al., 1998). The original study was conducted using the ACE Checklist, a 10-item questionnaire designed to be completed by adults who reflect on their experiences in childhood. Participants were asked to endorse whether they had experienced a series of 10 events. Five questions specifically focus on types of abuse and neglect: emotional abuse, physical abuse, sexual abuse, emotional neglect, and physical neglect. The remaining five questions assess an individual's experience of household dysfunction: mother treated violently, household substance abuse, household mental illness, parental separation or divorce, and incarcerated household member.

The ACE Checklist is commonly used as a screening tool by providers across multiple settings and is often used by clinicians to determine whether a child should receive a more comprehensive trauma-informed assessment (Felitti et al., 1998). Some critiques of the ACE Checklist for this purpose include that it was originally designed for a research study, not as a screening tool, and it was not designed to be completed by children. Furthermore, it includes only a subset of types of trauma that an individual may experience, and it does not gather information on ensuing symptoms or reactions (Finkelhor, 2018). There have been multiple adaptations to the ACE Checklist that address some of these concerns; a link to a list of adapted ACE tools can be found in Appendix A.

Developmental History

The impact of child trauma exposure on brain development has become firmly established in recent years (De Bellis & Zisk, 2014). Therefore, it is important to explore the relationship between a child's experiences of trauma and their physical, cognitive, and emotional development. This information may often be gathered during the context of a clinical interview, as described in Chapter 3. However, in some circumstances, it may be appropriate to conduct a more thorough developmental assessment incorporating the use of assessment tools. An overview of tools specific to a comprehensive developmental assessment is outside the scope of this book, and clinicians are encouraged to ask caregivers about the child's developmental milestones at the first visit. Clinicians are also encouraged to use other development-specific assessment tools to explore other types of development, including attachment, which is of particular importance in the trauma-informed assessment process. Appendix A includes a link to additional resources on developmental assessment.

Trauma Responses

Beyond trauma exposure, there are several tools designed to assess a child's responses to the trauma they have experienced. Some tools focus specifically on assessing posttraumatic stress reactions, whereas others are broader and assess for complex trauma reactions. These tools are described below and listed in Table 5.1.

Posttraumatic Stress Reactions. There are several tools that can be particularly helpful from a diagnostic perspective in helping the clinician determine whether a child meets the diagnostic criteria for posttraumatic stress or other disorders. These tools tend to be longer, structured interview processes in which the clinician gathers a comprehensive set of information that can specifically pinpoint diagnostic considerations. Some commonly used tools include the PTSD in Preschool Aged Children scale (Levendosky et al., 2002); the Clinician-Administered PTSD Scale for *DSM-5* (*Diagnostic and Statistical Manual of Mental Disorders*, fifth ed.; American Psychiatric Association, 2013), Child and Adolescent Version (Pynoos et al., 2015); the Children's PTSD Inventory (Saigh, 2004); and the PTSD Semi-Structured Interview and Observational Record (Scheeringa & Zeanah, 1994). These tools generally include questions related to the child's trauma exposure, as well as questions designed to determine whether the child is specifically experiencing PTSD symptoms. Table 5.1 provides information on these tools.

Complex Trauma Reactions. As described in Chapter 3, children and adolescents may exhibit certain behaviors and responses following exposure to trauma that are broader than PTSD symptoms. There are several tools that are designed to assess for a broader range of traumatic stress reactions, including the Adolescent Dissociative Experiences Scale (Armstrong et al., 1997), the TSCC (Briere, 1996), the TSCYC (Briere, 2005), the Child Sexual Behavior Inventory (Friedrich, 1997), and the Child Dissociative Checklist (Putnam et al., 1993). These tools often assess for a range of behaviors and responses that the child may exhibit following trauma, including

- changes in ability to regulate mood;
- externalizing and internalizing behavior problems;
- changes in attention, concentration, learning, or other cognitive processes;
- headaches, stomachaches, or other somatic complaints;
- inability to form attachments and maintain positive relationships;
- dysregulated sleeping, eating, or other physiological responses; and
- evidence of dissociation following the child's exposure to trauma.

These types of tools provide the clinician with rich information regarding the child's broader symptoms that may have resulted from the trauma while assisting with treatment planning efforts. Table 5.1 provides information on these tools.

Although there is consensus among researchers and practitioners that children and adolescents may experience complex trauma reactions beyond PTSD (A. Cook et al., 2005; see Chapter 3 for more information), there are few tools designed to assess the presence of complex trauma symptoms among children and adolescents in a single tool. One semistructured interview tool, the Structured Interview for Disorders of Extreme Stress (SIDES; Pelcovitz et al., 1997), was originally developed to assess for the presence or absence and severity of a range of complex trauma symptoms and responses in adults. The SIDES has been adapted for use with adolescents as well (SIDES–Adolescent version; Habib et al., 2005).

More recently, leaders in the field of complex developmental trauma in childhood have proposed that complex trauma reactions can be conceptualized as a potentially new diagnosis, "developmental trauma disorder" (DTD; van der Kolk, 2005; van der Kolk et al., 2019). These authors have proposed that DTD includes four criteria, each of which may be measured using related tools in order to determine whether a child or adolescent is experiencing complex trauma reactions:

1. *Criterion A:* Exposure to relational trauma and/or attachment difficulties, which may be measured using the tools described earlier in this chapter on assessing trauma exposure

2. *Criterion B:* Current emotional or somatic dysregulation, which may be measured using the Five Factor Personality Inventory–Children (Kroes et al., 2005) and the Affect Intensity and Reactivity Measure for Youth (R. E. Jones et al., 2009; see Ford, 2011, for more measures)

3. *Criterion C:* Current attentional or behavioral dysregulation, which may be measured using the Child Behavior Checklist (CBCL; Achenbach & Rescorla, 2001), the TSCC (Briere, 1996), and the TSCYC (Briere, 2005)

4. *Criterion D:* Current relational or self-dysregulation, which may be measured using the CBCL (Achenbach & Rescorla, 2001) and the Children's Depression Inventory (Kovacs, 1992), among others

An additional instrument, the Developmental Trauma Disorder Semi-Structured Interview (Ford et al., 2018), is designed specifically to determine whether a child or adolescent meets the criteria for DTD. Information on this measure is included in Table 5.1.

Functional Difficulties and Risk Behaviors. Research has suggested that mental health symptoms and functional outcomes may be even more common than PTSD responses among children (Briere & Spinazzola, 2009; Hawkins & Radcliffe, 2006; Ohan et al., 2002), particularly following exposure to complex or chronic interpersonal trauma (Briere & Spinazzola, 2009; Courtois, 2004; Kisiel, Fehrenbach, et al., 2009). *Functional difficulties* typically refers to the negative impact of trauma exposure on the child's or adolescent's functioning across multiple domains, including home, school, and relationships. Tools examining a child's or adolescent's functioning broadly can be paired with trauma-specific measures to create a picture of the child or adolescent and their relationships, behaviors, and concerns. Some of the more commonly used tools include the CBCL (Achenbach & Rescorla, 2001) and the Child and Adolescent Needs and Strengths (CANS)–Trauma Comprehensive Version (Kisiel et al., 2013). These tools may also be used to assess the child's educational history and functioning, including special education services, and other education-related needs or concerns. These tools assist the clinician not only in gathering information on the child's traumatic stress reactions, but also in understanding at a deeper level how those reactions are impacting the child's daily functioning. Information on these tools is presented in Table 5.1.

Given the co-occurrence of trauma exposure with potential risk factors, it is also important to consider incorporating the assessment of risk factors into any trauma-informed assessment process for children and adolescents. Clinicians are encouraged to assess risk factors such as suicidality and other types of self-harm, danger to others, running away, sexual aggression, sexually reactive behaviors, other types of intentional misbehavior, and delinquency. The CANS–Trauma Comprehensive (Kisiel et al., 2013) has a specific domain focused on a range of risk behaviors. Other commonly used tools include the Structured Assessment of Violence Risk in Youth (Borum et al., 2006) and the Child and Adolescent Risk and Needs Evaluation (Seifert, 2007).

Perceptions and Attributions About Trauma. Another area of interest for clinicians is gathering information on the child's or adolescent's perceptions and attributions about the trauma they have experienced. There are some scales that focus broadly on a child's or adolescent's experiences of blame or shame. Some of the commonly used tools include the Shame and Guilt scales of the Test of Self-Conscious Affect–Adolescent (Watson et al., 2016). Other tools look more specifically at a child's attributional style, including the Children's Attributional Style Questionnaire–Revised (Kaslow, 2000) and the Children's Attributions and Perceptions Scale (Mannarino et al., 1994).

Subtypes of Trauma Response.
Complicated grief reactions. As highlighted in Chapter 3, a child or adolescent may experience symptoms of traumatic grief following the loss of a significant person in their life. Some of the tools that assess for complex trauma reactions can also assist in identifying specific issues related to trauma and grief, but there are other tools designed specifically for this type of trauma, such as the Traumatic Grief Inventory (Boelen & Smid, 2017).

Disaster responses. In most cases, the process of using tools in the assessment of disaster responses would be similar to that of assessing for responses to other types of traumatic events. However, there are some tools that are specifically designed to assess for individual disaster responses among youth. One commonly used tool designed to measure the presence of PTSD symptoms in children and adolescents after a hurricane is the Kauai Recovery Index (KRI; Hamada et al., 2003). The KRI was specifically designed for use after community-wide disasters. More information on the KRI is included in Table 5.1.

Family and Caregiver Trauma History and Functioning
Although it is important to gather information on the child's or adolescent's experience of trauma and subsequent functioning, it can also be helpful to gather information on the caregiver's trauma and loss history and functioning as part of the trauma-informed assessment. Understanding more about the caregiver's trauma history can provide the clinician with important information on how the caregiver may be responding to the child's experiences, particularly if the caregiver has experienced a similar type of trauma (e.g., sexual abuse) or if the child and caregiver are experiencing the trauma together but with distinct perspectives (e.g., domestic violence). Integrating caregiver-specific tools into the larger assessment process can provide unique information about the caregiver's capacity to provide support and willingness to engage in services.

There are several tools that are specifically designed to gather information on an adult's or caregiver's trauma history. These tools can be integrated into the trauma-informed assessment process with children and adolescents. Tools specifically designed to assess for an adult's history of trauma include the Trauma Screening Questionnaire (Brewin et al., 2002) and the Primary Care PTSD Screen for *DSM-5* (Prins et al., 2015).

Another component of the trauma-informed assessment process is examining the caregiver's trauma reactions and overall functioning, as the caregiver is often the primary source of support for the child and can support or impede the child's progress in treatment. Some tools are designed specifically to assess caregiver functioning in order to understand any potential or ongoing safety concerns and mental health needs of caregivers, determine their capacity to support their child and the child's recovery from trauma, and identify any need for services for caregivers (Conradi et al., 2011; Kisiel, Blaustein, et al., 2009). Tools specifically designed to gather information on adults' trauma reactions include the Trauma Symptom Inventory (Briere, 1995) and the Detailed Assessment of Posttraumatic Stress (Briere, 2001). One example of a tool that assesses family and caregiver functioning is the CANS–Trauma Comprehensive (Kisiel et al., 2013). A link to information regarding a comprehensive review of caregiver assessment tools is in Appendix A.

Strengths

An essential part of a trauma-informed assessment sometimes overlooked is strengths or resilience in the child, caregiver, family, and community. Paying attention to strengths during the assessment process—including individual, caregiver, family, and broader environmental strengths—serves many purposes. There are multiple assessment tools that are designed to assess for child or caregiver strengths and resilience. Some focus on assessing for protective factors, some focus more broadly on strengths, and others assess the domains related to resilience. Sometimes it can be difficult for caregivers to think of strengths for their children, particularly when they are managing difficult behaviors related to trauma exposure. Therefore, a structured interview or use of a self-report tool focused on child strengths can be a way in which the clinician can gather information on a child's strengths in a unified way. A list of tools specifically designed to measure resilience, protective factors, and strengths in children and adolescents and adults, including caregivers, is located in Appendix A.

CHALLENGES AND PRACTICAL CONSIDERATIONS FOR CLINICIANS

With the increased focus on the use of trauma-focused assessment tools for youth and adults over the past 20 years, there has been a growth in the development of tools for various types of child trauma and their subsequent effects. The challenge for clinicians is in identifying the tools that would be the most useful for the youth and families they serve, taking into account multiple considerations such as the cost of the tools, age and developmental stage of the youth, languages available, research conducted on the tools, type of training necessary to use the tools, and type of information provided by the tools.

The task of selecting tools and using them consistently and in a thoughtful way in practice can be overwhelming, particularly if the clinician is not working within a system, such as a mental health agency, that can offer support for these efforts. Furthermore, although a larger agency may have additional resources to put toward purchasing and implementing trauma-informed assessment tools, there may still be restrictions on the agency's resources and capacity. For example, mental health agencies are increasingly being asked to assess for challenges such as depression, anxiety, and hyperactivity, among other needs. Therefore, identifying a core set of tools that can be administered across an agency without overburdening either the clinicians or the children and families can be challenging. As discussed in Chapter 3, it is recommended that the agency and clinicians review the populations served and prioritize their most pressing concerns and service needs. Creating a core group of a few assessment measures to administer to all youth and families in addition to supplementary measures to administer to clients with specific needs can be a helpful structure in which to integrate multiple assessments without overwhelming clinicians or the broader agency system (Chadwick Center for Children and Families, 2009).

However, as noted at the beginning of this chapter, an even bigger challenge may be the inconsistent use of standardized or evidence-based assessment tools in clinical practice. Previous studies unfortunately have suggested that standardized measures are inconsistently and rarely used in clinical practice (Cashel, 2002; J. R. Cook et al., 2017; Ionita & Fitzpatrick, 2014). Yet sole use of unstandardized tools to the exclusion of standardized tools or reliable and valid techniques can compromise the reliability of the information collected and lead to misidentifying the primary disorder or diagnosis and the intervention or treatment approach that may be most appropriate to the child's symptom profile (J. R. Cook et al., 2017).

Additional challenges may exist in terms of the types of tools selected for a trauma-informed assessment given the wide range of symptoms that children can manifest in response to trauma. For instance, as initially noted in Chapter 3, when using PTSD assessments alone, clinicians may miss the broader set of responses that youth may exhibit (i.e., in addition to PTSD symptoms). Studies using measures of PTSD have emphasized the wide range of symptoms and comorbid diagnoses that often accompany post-traumatic disorders, such as depressive and anxiety disorders, substance use disorders, and oppositional defiant and conduct disorders, which may also be prevalent among those diagnosed with PTSD (Foa, Keane, & Friedman, 2000; Newman et al., 1996). These diagnoses can encompass many of the complex trauma responses noted above. As initially described in Chapter 3, it is important to use a trauma lens when exploring the range of potential diagnoses in youth impacted by trauma; for instance, these diagnoses can be interpreted as possible complex trauma responses. This understanding can help support trauma-informed treatment planning efforts by ensuring that these disorders are not addressed in isolation in the context of treatment planning and intervention, which are discussed more fully in Chapter 6.

In terms of assessment across different age groups, there may not always be established measures or tools to assess key domains based on age. This is where the use of a multimethod approach becomes important. Although use of standardized tools is critical, it is important to supplement the gathering of information with behavioral observation or use of a clinical interview, particularly when tools are not available or useful for assessing certain domains for a given age group. These techniques can be used more flexibly to support information gathering across different areas, to collect further details in relation to certain domains, and to contribute to a comprehensive picture of the child and family.

CONCLUSION

There are a multitude of tools that exist for a trauma-informed assessment. These include measures for children and adolescents designed to identify exposure to a specific traumatic event, exposure to multiple traumatic events, and reactions to trauma and subsequent challenges with functioning and relationships across settings. Although clinicians often believe that their clinical interview provides enough information to support treatment planning efforts, research has suggested that clinicians are not nearly as accurate in identifying areas of need in the context of a clinical interview as when they use quantitative assessment measures (Meehl, 1996). Therefore, the integration of standardized, trauma-informed assessment tools into the broader assessment process is essential in gathering crucial information to inform treatment planning efforts. Use of tools that meet the specific needs of the population served and that account for age, developmental stage, and culture while also having a solid research base can serve as an effective strategy for gathering meaningful information and directing treatment planning efforts.

6 COLLABORATIVE AND MEANINGFUL APPLICATIONS OF TRAUMA-INFORMED ASSESSMENT

Previous chapters discussed the key domains and essential processes elements of conducting a comprehensive trauma-informed assessment. Another central, but often overlooked, aspect of the trauma-informed assessment process is the collaborative and meaningful application of the assessment results. This chapter discusses the importance of meaningfully applying and translating assessment findings in practice with youth and family members, as well as for providers working with the family across various service systems. Collaboration and meaningful application of assessment results is referred to in different terms; collaboration with a youth and family in the context of mental health treatment is often referred to as "engagement," whereas this process at the program level is commonly referred to as "teaming" and at the system level is often called "system integration" (Taylor & Siegfried, 2005). This chapter reviews the importance of promoting family engagement in the assessment process and core competencies for addressing family engagement, enhancing the information integration process to inform collaborative treatment planning and provision of appropriate services to youth and families, and bolstering provider collaboration across systems through trauma-informed

https://doi.org/10.1037/0000233-006

Trauma-Informed Assessment With Children and Adolescents: Strategies to Support Clinicians, by C. Kisiel, T. Fehrenbach, L. Conradi, and L. Weil

assessment by sharing relevant information and enabling all providers to have a shared understanding of a youth's functioning, strengths, and needs.

FAMILY ENGAGEMENT IN THE ASSESSMENT PROCESS

As introduced in Chapter 3, engaging the youth and family is a crucial aspect of the comprehensive trauma-informed assessment process. The term *assessment translation* is used to describe the process by which assessment information can be discussed and used as a part of collaborative and meaningful practice with families and providers (Kisiel, Conradi, et al., 2014). Assessment translation with families is essential as much of the information gathered through the assessment process may be novel for the youth and family. Furthermore, conceptualizing the assessment process as person-centered emphasizes the importance of the assessment experience as a collaborative process between the clinician and the youth and family, in which all members of the team are equal partners in both the assessment and subsequent treatment planning process (Lyons & Israel, 2018).

The literature has emphasized the need for increased engagement of youth and families in the assessment process (Kisiel, Conradi, et al., 2014). It is well established that low family engagement in both prevention and intervention services contributes to high rates of service dropout (Gomby, 2000; Gopalan et al., 2010; Masi et al., 2003; McKay et al., 2004; National Institute of Mental Health, 2001). Unfortunately, some evidence also suggests that individuals with a high need for services because of their symptoms or psychosocial stressors have a higher likelihood of ceasing services early (Snell-Johns et al., 2004).

As the assessment process may be the first or an early point of contact with service providers, it is essential to prioritize family engagement during these early interactions in order to facilitate ongoing involvement in services after the initial assessment concludes. Integrating the family into the treatment process and increasing family coping have both been shown to improve engagement in treatment (Gopalan et al., 2010; Ingoldsby, 2010; McKay et al., 2004). Thus, early emphasis on establishing open communication and building a trusting relationship can help providers be more effective in working with youth and their families. Furthermore, youth and families often have a good understanding of adjustments that can improve their current functioning or quality of life or have a unique perspective on current challenges that may arise through the assessment process only by eliciting this information directly from families (Finello, 2011; Kisiel, Torgersen, et al., 2018).

Additionally, encouraging and supporting the youth and family to be active members in the assessment process and equal collaborators in the treatment planning process increases clinicians' understanding of both the youth and family as well as the rationale for the next steps in treatment; this understanding allows individuals to be more active in their own care (Carman et al., 2013). Thus, engaging family members as key stakeholders or partners from the outset of the initial assessment contributes to empowerment of the youth and family and can mitigate retention challenges and contribute to positive therapeutic outcomes (Kisiel, Torgersen, et al., 2018). Additionally, family engagement in the assessment process has also been linked to caregiver satisfaction, bolstered by the experience of feeling that they can have their questions and concerns adequately addressed through the assessment process (Tharinger et al., 2009). The assessment process marks the beginning phase of treatment, and the trust and alliance developed during this process can greatly influence a youth's and family's motivation to engage in further treatment.

Strategies for effectively engaging the family in the assessment process include working with the family to schedule the assessment at a time that is convenient for them and giving them control over the order of the assessment process (e.g., begin with the clinical interview and then complete the standardized measures, or vice versa). Providing families with some control over the situation may alleviate anxiety that can accompany engaging in services with a new agency and answering a number of very personal questions. Once the information is gathered, it is important to actively integrate the child and caregiver into discussions about what will happen next, sharing information in multiple ways so that the child and family are well aware of the next steps for treatment.

A couple of important areas to consider when first involving family members in the assessment process are the age of the child or adolescent and the family dynamics. As highlighted in other chapters, the age of the youth will affect the structure of the assessment process and how assessment information is gathered. Additionally, the youth's level of engagement in the assessment process, the sharing of feedback with the youth and family, and the treatment planning processes will also need to be tailored to the chronological and developmental age of the youth to ensure that the information being both gathered from and shared with the youth is appropriate (see Chapters 2 and 3 for further information on this topic). Additionally, deciding which family members to include as key partners in the assessment process may depend on the unique dynamics of the family and how each member has been impacted by the traumatic event (de Arellano &

Danielson, 2008). As is described in Chapter 4, when assessing transnational youth who immigrated from other countries, clinicians should consider whether there are important family members (e.g., primary caregivers) still living in the country of origin who can be reached by telephone or video (Falicov, 2007); this may be of particular importance for unaccompanied minors. Thus, it is important for the clinician to understand the family system in order to determine which family members are appropriate to engage in the process given these unique relationships.

The clinician will ideally use assessment results to formulate treatment goals together with the youth and family (Kisiel, Torgersen, et al., 2018). By setting goals together, the youth and family can have a sense of ownership in the treatment process. In addition, this collaboration supports the child and caregiver in monitoring changes and improvements and adjusting plans together as needed over time. Engaging the youth and family in establishing treatment goals is also likely to increase motivation and reduce resistance, cancellations, and no-show appointments (Hawley & Weisz, 2005). Clinicians who conduct assessments with families who are also engaged in the child welfare system could consider seeking the family's approval for sharing the results of the assessment with other providers in that system in order to increase coordination of care and trauma-informed service planning. These steps are central to engaging in the process of collaborative service and treatment planning with family members and developing assessment-driven treatment goals that are responsive to needs (Kisiel, Conradi, et al., 2014; Kisiel, Torgersen, et al., 2018; Lyons, 2004).

CORE COMPETENCIES OF FAMILY ENGAGEMENT IN THE ASSESSMENT PROCESS

Engaging youth and families during and after the assessment process is not always an easy task. As assessment translation is a relatively new concept, even youth and families who have received prior assessments and services may be unfamiliar with the process of being asked to engage in and collaborate in the assessment, goal setting, and treatment planning processes. Four core competencies have been identified for approaching the development of collaborative relationships with families during the trauma-informed assessment process:

1. explaining the purpose of the assessment and how the assessment results will be used in the context of decision making about services,

2. providing trauma-informed psychoeducation to the youth and family,

3. sharing results of the assessment with the family and engaging the family in developing treatment and service planning goals, and

4. continuing to share progress with families over time and collaborating with family members to make adjustments to the treatment plan depending on changing areas of needs and strength (Kisiel, Torgersen, et al., 2018).

The various ways that providers can approach each of these competency areas are further detailed below.

Explaining the Purpose of the Assessment

First, it is essential to be open and transparent with the youth and family members about the reason for the assessment process as a whole by providing a youth- and family-friendly rationale and describing the purpose of using a range of assessment techniques including interviews, behavioral observations, and different assessment and screening tools. The rationale provided to families should include a description of how these assessment tools can inform the development of treatment goals and the provision of services. Transparency throughout each step of the assessment process allows for the creation of trust, and feeling well-informed may empower families to be more active in the assessment and treatment process (see the Key Principles of a Trauma-Informed Approach section in Chapter 2 for further information). Given the amount of information that is gathered from and shared with the youth and family during the assessment process, it is essential that the provider regularly check in with the family about their understanding of the process and the information shared and allow the family flexibility to direct the provider with regard to how much information they need or want about the process.

Providing Trauma-Informed Psychoeducation

Second, using the assessment process as an avenue for offering psycho-education or education about the effects of trauma allows the family to better understand the child's and family's needs and strengths in relation to their trauma history and across a variety of domains (Kisiel, Torgersen, et al., 2018). Whereas psychoeducation is a formalized practice that can be applied in conjunction with psychotherapy (see Cummings & Cummings, 2008), the term "psychoeducation" has been widely used and adapted in a less formalized manner within mental health settings. In this regard, it is important to note that this term can sometimes be considered pejorative or patronizing, based on feedback from caregivers. Information gathered during caregiver focus groups suggested that when working with families, providers should consider using the terms "education" or "shared understanding" when referring to the translation of trauma-related symptoms and needs with family members; these terms may be preferred when trying to equalize and facilitate communication between providers and families (Center for Child Trauma Assessment and Service Planning, 2014).

Increasing knowledge about trauma and its impact can facilitate a shared understanding between family and providers and foster a common language about the youth's needs, which can be integrated throughout the treatment process. Moreover, in relation to children and families exposed to trauma, it may be particularly helpful to provide information about normal reactions to trauma, discuss the need for support and referral for services for other members of the family (e.g., siblings, caregivers) who are also affected by the trauma, and collaborate with community partners (e.g., child welfare, law enforcement, schools) to ensure access to community-based resources and services for children who need them the most. Because comprehensive trauma-informed assessment is a critical component of the intervention process, providing education about trauma also serves as a logical vehicle for clarifying the rationale for assessment and treatment, addressing concerns, sharing relevant information, communicating expectations, and demystifying the therapeutic process.

Finally, this psychoeducation process can increase the youth's and family's buy-in to the intervention process. Rather than being directed about what they will be working on and how they will be doing so, this process encourages open communication in which youth and families are empowered to voice their point of view, express their feelings, ask questions, and help make decisions throughout the process along with the provider. For instance, clinicians can engage family members in a discussion about how a youth is experiencing a range of difficulties (such as posttraumatic symptoms, risk behaviors, and functional difficulties), which may be connected to and ways of responding to their trauma experiences. Family members and youth can benefit from learning about how these symptoms may fluctuate over time in responses to stressors, triggers, or changes in development. Enhancing knowledge about trauma may normalize these responses for youth and caregivers, empower the family to better understand why the youth may be responding in this way (which may previously have felt out of their control), and help them begin to identify ways to interrupt these negative response patterns and to find healthier ways of coping.

Sharing Results and Facilitating Collaborative Treatment Planning

To effectively explain the results of a trauma-informed assessment to the youth and family, clinicians must first have a strong foundational knowledge of child trauma and its effects. This knowledge base will allow clinicians to convey information to families in a way that is digestible and may allow clinicians to explain concepts in several different ways to ensure that the youth and family fully understand the assessment results. Furthermore, as a comprehensive trauma-informed assessment process gathers information across a variety of areas of strength and need (and potentially from different time points in a youth's life, if previous assessments have been conducted) and integrates information from multiple sources, the meaningful application of these data requires providers to integrate this information into a trauma-informed case conceptualization in a way that makes sense.

When a provider has a solid understanding of the assessment data and a strong case formulation, they can explain the results of the assessment to the family in a cohesive way. For example, rather than reviewing clinically elevated items from different screening and assessment measures, a more effective review of the assessment results would, ideally, integrate this information and present the data as a narrative. For instance, rather than explaining that a child received a score of 70 on an assessment, the clinician might offer a more comprehensive, narrative picture of the score, such as, "This score supports what you mentioned seeing at home, as the child's presentation suggests that they struggle to keep things organized both at home and at school." Furthermore, the clinician can help both the family and other providers better understand the possible connection between a youth's trauma experiences and various trauma reactions.

The amount and type of information shared with the child or adolescent should be determined on the basis of the child's developmental age, so information may be quite basic and limited with very young children. The youth and caregivers often spend a great deal of time completing the assessment measures and may need to be encouraged to do so (e.g., reminded of the purpose of the assessment along the way). Therefore, they will likely be invested in understanding the results given this time commitment. In particular, including a range of perspectives in the assessment process (e.g., child, parent, teachers) and sharing feedback with families in a manner that is sensitive to their needs and priorities, such as by validating their experiences, instilling a sense of hope, and highlighting their strengths, can help normalize these responses and reassure them that the impact of trauma on their lives is understood and can be addressed (Cohen et al., 2006). For instance, when presenting assessment results, an effective method for engaging families is for the clinician to connect assessment findings back to particular examples families provided, noting how the findings may support what family members are seeing or experiencing. This approach can help solidify and bring to light the assessment information. Providing feedback in an appropriate way is crucial to setting the tone of therapy, opening the lines of communication about the treatment process and treatment planning, and increasing youth and family buy-in to treatment.

Comprehension of the assessment results is a crucial step toward a family's ability to fully understand the need for treatment and engage in the treatment planning process and, equally importantly, to feel like an equal partner in this process. As discussed in Chapters 3 and 5, if a clinician's understanding of the assessment results differs from a youth's or family's understanding, this can result in challenges both with the alliance and trust between the family and clinician and with the family's understanding of how to proceed with the next steps in the treatment or service planning process (The John Praed Foundation, 2015). Conversely, engaging family members effectively and early in the assessment process enables the family to feel that their voices are being heard and their sentiments are truly influencing later discussions of treatment recommendations (Bailey & Powell, 2005).

The way in which data gathered during the assessment are shared with families is essential to ensuring there is understanding and alignment between providers and families. Some clinicians may be inclined to share data points or verbatim responses to questions. However, a potentially more effective approach to translation of assessment findings is for a clinician to synthesize the data collected during the assessment process and create a case conceptualization that includes concrete examples supporting the clinician's hypotheses. For example, the clinician may start by providing the family with a reminder of the reason for referral and review the different components that went into the assessment process (i.e., interviews, obser-vation, standardized measures, and any historical assessment data that may exist). The clinician can then provide a high-level overview of findings regard-ing the youth's functioning across settings (e.g., school, home). Once the family has an understanding of the bigger picture, the clinician can then move on to more specific areas of needs and strengths. This process allows the clinician to share information in a way that is relatable and relevant for family members, rather than asking family members to connect many different data points across various assessment approaches and domains or areas of assessment.

As mentioned earlier, it is important that families be given the oppor-tunity to reach and share their own conceptualizations with the provider; however, many families may be hesitant to do so, and thus this should not be expected. If the family's perception differs from the clinician's perspective, it should still be valued and continue to be examined over time. When establishing clinical hypotheses, the clinician should consider alternative explanations for the problem areas identified, inviting the family to question, challenge, or add to the conceptualization while also remembering and helping the family understand that hypotheses are not static and may change over time throughout the duration of the treatment process.

Providing assessment feedback in a thoughtful and appropriate manner sets the tone for therapy and other services moving forward; this also allows both clinicians and families to feel confident in their conceptualization and comfortable asking clarifying questions. Part of assessment translation is the provider determining the most effective way to present and share information with families so that the assessment results are easy to read and understand. This may require providers to use visuals or visually appealing reports.

Once the family and youth (if appropriate given chronological and developmental age) have a solid understanding of the assessment results, the clinician can facilitate collaboration with families to establish treatment goals, as initially described in Chapter 3, and to select the appropriate treatment modality (e.g., individual, family, group) and treatment focus (e.g., posttraumatic stress disorder [PTSD], depression, or attention problems; difficulties with attachment and peer relationships). Involving the youth and family in the process of identifying the treatment approach and goals allows all individuals the ability to feel ownership and buy-in to the treatment process (Hawley & Weisz, 2005). Alternately, the lack of involvement of the youth and family in the treatment and service planning process may lead to some youth and families receiving services that are not effective or appropriate or that are even potentially detrimental; thus, if family members, as key partners, are not provided with information about the assessment process and findings, this can place the youth and family at a disadvantage (Kisiel, Torgersen, et al., 2018).

When setting treatment goals, it is important to keep in mind that the treatment plan is two tiered. The primary purpose of the treatment plan is to reduce symptoms and eliminate identified areas of concern that have been identified as priorities throughout the assessment process. The secondary, yet equally important and closely linked, objective is for the child to experience resolution related to the trauma or traumas that brought them into treatment, as well as to foster healthy growth and development and build strengths. As part of this secondary process, the youth and family will ideally gain further understanding of the impact of the trauma experiences; make links among attributions, behaviors, and emotions; and gain skills in areas such as safety, socialization, and communication (Chadwick Center for Children and Families, 2009).

When approached in a meaningful and collaborative way, the assessment process enables family members to gain an increased understanding of a youth's strengths, needs, and current functioning, which may facilitate improved transactional patterns within the family through the caregivers' new understanding (Tharinger et al., 2009). Thus, families may be able to experience some therapeutic benefit from the assessment process alone even before treatment begins (Smith, 2010).

Continuing to Share Progress and Collaborate With Families

Last, it is important to consider that involving families is essential not only during the initial assessment but also in all iterative and ongoing aspects of the assessment process. The treatment plan is not static, and as such, sharing progress with families and collaboratively discussing potential adjustments to treatment goals and services (informed by the reassessment process) as needed bolsters the ongoing collaboration between service providers and the youth and family (Kisiel, Torgersen, et al., 2018). The use of reports with simple visual graphics that track changes over time can be a useful way to engage families in this discussion and highlight areas of growth and continued areas of need. Additionally, measuring change over time and sharing feedback on the results of the assessment may enhance a youth's and family's feelings of self-efficacy and improvement that can further contribute to their ongoing buy-in to the treatment process (Child Welfare Information Gateway, 2016).

USE OF TRAUMA-INFORMED ASSESSMENT TO BOLSTER MULTIDISCIPLINARY COLLABORATION ACROSS SYSTEMS

The trauma-informed assessment process is also a helpful avenue for supporting communication and collaboration across multidisciplinary providers who are supporting the youth's and family's care across various service systems (e.g., behavioral health, child welfare, juvenile justice, education). Collaborating during the assessment process allows the clinician to gather information from other service providers working with the youth and family. Gathering information from each of these providers can allow for a clearer and more holistic understanding of the current functioning, strengths, and areas of need of the youth and family and can assist the family by helping the clinician identify any inconsistencies in case conceptualization or symptom presentations across different settings or overlap in services required by each system.

Providers in certain settings may have a better understanding of a youth's or family's functioning in specific domains, which can help the clinician establish a more accurate picture of the youth's functioning across domains and settings. For example, teachers may have a better understanding of academic and social functioning at school, whereas if a youth is already receiving therapeutic services, the therapist may have a stronger sense of the youth's current mental health and traumatic stress symptoms. It is difficult to create targeted goals for a youth that effectively meet their needs without having a solid understanding of the youth's internal experience and functioning across settings (Kisiel, Torgersen, et al., 2018).

Additionally, reviewing both the screening results (if available) and the information derived from the assessment process with providers across systems (including the referral source) can facilitate communication across settings and systems (Kisiel, Torgersen, et al., 2018). As noted earlier in this book, it is especially pertinent for clinicians conducting the assessment to share the results with treatment providers if the clinician completing the assessment is not the one who will be providing the youth or family with therapeutic services. Information sharing should always be done within the bounds of confidentiality, so some clinicians may be worried about sharing this information, including how much information to share and how it will be used. However, the results from the assessment process can play a critical part in ensuring that the child receives appropriate services. For example, if the child was referred for services by child welfare, sharing information on the results of the assessment process can provide critical information that can assist the child welfare worker in gathering an accurate and comprehensive picture of what the child has experienced and how it may be impacting the child's functioning and in creating a service plan that is trauma informed and can address the unique needs of the child. Effectively sharing assessment feedback with providers across various systems requires that the clinician discuss and translate assessment findings in multiple ways depending on the knowledge base and background of the provider receiving the assessment information (Mercer, 2011).

The information-sharing step is crucial because all service providers having the same information leads to richer conversations about service recommendations and referrals. When service providers across systems have shared knowledge about the impact of trauma and the range of potential trauma responses that youth may exhibit, they are better informed to collaborate and effectively communicate about goals, service planning, and progress for youth and their families.

As with families, creating a shared understanding across providers supports effective communication and service delivery. Sometimes creating this understanding entails offering education to providers about the range of trauma-related needs (beyond PTSD) and advocating for the use of a trauma-informed approach across different systems. Streamlined communication and shared understanding about a youth's and family's needs, strengths, and treatment and service goals can support providers in effectively addressing the youth's and family's needs and better ensuring appropriate execution of the treatment or service plan (Lyons & Israel, 2018). Sharing and translating information and feedback from the trauma-informed assessment process with providers working in different systems also increases the potential for informing and supporting trauma-informed care for youth who are served across multiple systems.

As with collaborative and meaningful application of the assessment process with families, it is also essential that communication across providers and service systems continues after the assessment process ends. Continuing to stay connected and having ongoing discussions about a youth's progress will help all providers with the process of adapting and refining a youth's and family's treatment and service goals and plans throughout the duration of services.

CONCLUSION

Conducting a comprehensive trauma-informed assessment requires knowledge of essential process elements, key domains, and components. Another critical piece of the assessment process is how results are translated, shared, and applied with both family members and other providers in order to best support the needs of the individual youth and family. The assessment translation process can set the stage for an effective and more meaningful intervention process as well when this level of engagement with families occurs from the outset of services. Unfortunately, this crucial portion of the assessment process if often overlooked. When assessment results are effectively translated and shared with both families and all providers involved in a youth's care (within an agency and across systems), it allows opportunities for the family and providers to develop a common language and shared vision for the youth and family and their path forward and to advocate for trauma-informed care across the systems where youth and families are served. This form of collaboration can increase buy-in and alignment between providers and families, which are needed to ensure that a youth's needs are adequately addressed through the process of trauma-informed treatment.

7 CONCLUSIONS AND FUTURE DIRECTIONS

When conducting a comprehensive trauma-informed assessment, it is critical that clinicians consider the various components of a trauma-informed assessment framework (as outlined in Chapter 1). This framework includes embedding a series of essential process elements as foundational to this process and using key domains and techniques to structure the assessment. Furthermore, it is important that clinicians are aware of and know how to make adjustments for sociocultural differences and that they strive to stay educated regarding the availability of assessment tools and ways to select the most appropriate ones for each child and family. Clinicians must also be committed to engaging and working collaboratively as partners with children and families throughout the assessment process, from start to finish.

The chapters in this book, both broad and detailed, are filled with practical recommendations and concrete suggestions for clinicians. For the benefit of readers, we highlight the key recommendations from each chapter in the next section. In the Future Directions section that follows, we then consider how trauma-informed assessment research and practice can continue to evolve in order to be responsive to gaps in knowledge and service

https://doi.org/10.1037/0000233-007
Trauma-Informed Assessment With Children and Adolescents: Strategies to Support Clinicians, by C. Kisiel, T. Fehrenbach, L. Conradi, and L. Weil

delivery, especially during unprecedented situations such as the COVID-19 pandemic, which is occurring as this book is being published.

KEY RECOMMENDATIONS

Chapter 1 provides a definition and overview of trauma-informed assessment, describes the context and rationale for trauma-informed assessment, and highlights some of the key challenges associated with integrating this approach in practice within child-serving settings. This chapter introduces a framework for trauma-informed assessment and summarizes the aspects of this framework, which are designed to support the effective implementation of trauma-informed assessment in practice. Chapter 1 also offers a synopsis of the content and organization of the book, including the ways it is designed to address gaps in the field by offering a practical resource for clinicians on how to conduct a trauma-informed assessment.

Chapter 2 describes the importance of embedding trauma-informed assessment within a broader trauma-informed practice framework, such as the Substance Abuse and Mental Health Services Administration's (2014) key principles of a trauma-informed approach. Chapter 2 also describes six specific processes that are critical to implementing trauma-informed assessments: clinician training, the creation of an emotionally and physically safe environment, engagement of youth and families as active participants in the assessment, the use of assessment findings for case conceptualization and planning, the use of evidence-based tools and approaches, and reassessment over time as a method of tracking progress and adjusting treatment goals.

Chapter 3 provides guidance regarding the structure and content of the trauma-informed assessment. Key recommendations include the importance of assessing a number of key domains through a comprehensive assessment process. These domains include, but are not limited to, a child's lifetime exposure to trauma and loss experiences; a child's full range of trauma responses, including traumatic stress symptoms that fall within and outside of the diagnostic criteria of posttraumatic stress disorder; developmental history; functioning across a range of areas (including risk behaviors); family and caregiver trauma and loss history and family/caregiver functioning; and child, family, and community strengths. The information gathered as part of the trauma-informed assessment is ideally collected from a range of reporters including the child, caregivers, teachers, and other important adults who have frequent interaction with the child. Likewise, clinicians are strongly encouraged to use a variety of assessment techniques, including clinical interviews, standardized tools, and behavioral observations.

Chapter 3 also reinforces the importance of integrating and consolidating the range of assessment information gathered for use in practice. We recognize that incorporating and balancing all of the process and content recommendations in Chapters 2 and 3 can be challenging for providers who work in environments where they may encounter an array of time and resource constraints. Therefore, Chapter 3 also emphasizes the need to be flexible throughout the assessment approach and offers practical strategies and considerations for clinicians regarding how to balance competing demands.

Chapter 4 focuses on the importance of structuring and adapting the assessment process to best fit the developmental and sociocultural needs of youth and families. It identifies a range of intentional and unintentional barriers that can impact the amount and quality of the information provided by youth and families during the assessment process. It also highlights issues that may be of particular importance when working with specific populations (young children; adolescents; youth with developmental delays; system-involved youth; lesbian, gay, bisexual, transgender, and queer or questioning youth; people of color and Indigenous people; and immigrants and refugees). We provide recommendations that highlight the importance of clinicians proactively working to enhance their self-awareness regarding how their culture-specific beliefs, expectations, and biases may be played out during the assessment process. These recommendations are meant to inspire and motivate clinicians to learn as much as they can about the youth's and family's identity and cultural history so that clinicians can consider these factors and make creative and culturally responsive adaptations to the assessment process as needed.

Chapter 5 summarizes research and provides recommendations regarding the identification and implementation of specific tools as part of the trauma-informed assessment process. In addition to summarizing previously published reviews of assessment tools, Chapter 5 presents a table that describes 27 assessment tools that map onto the key domains of trauma-informed assessment highlighted in Chapter 3. This chapter is also highly beneficial for clinicians seeking guidance on how to select the best tools for the children and families they serve. Of particular importance are the sections on selecting tools that account for both the child's age and development and making sense of discrepant information collected from a variety of reporters and across a range of settings. Another useful contribution of this chapter is a list of key questions clinicians can consider when selecting the most appropriate trauma-informed assessment tools. This section specifically assists clinicians in weighing the importance of eight areas when making their choice of specific tools: purpose of the tool, supporting research, use with different populations and languages, cost, administration and scoring, ease of feedback, needs related to staff training, and ability to measure change over time.

The focus of Chapter 6 is on helping clinicians learn to build and apply assessment translation skills; this is a critical but still fairly new concept not fully addressed in other assessment resources or publications. In this chapter, clinicians are encouraged to think about the assessment process as the beginning stage of treatment, thereby calling special attention to the importance of meaningful family engagement starting at the point of first contact with the family and continuing throughout every step of the assessment process. As was mentioned in previous chapters, efforts to help children and families feel emotionally and physically safe during the assessment process are a critical aspect of building rapport, yet meaningful family engagement extends well beyond this aspect. For instance, Chapter 6 discusses the assessment process as the initial opportunity to validate, normalize, and provide families with psychoeducation regarding trauma-related needs, triggers, and the range of potential trauma responses.

Chapter 6 also highlights the benefits of sharing assessment results with family members in a digestible way and encourages clinicians to engage families as partners in collaborative treatment planning. This information sharing and collaboration may increase the likelihood that families obtain access to and decide to pursue and sustain their involvement in trauma-informed interventions over time. Helping families understand assessment as an iterative process, in which they are invited to work hand-in-hand with the clinician to monitor progress over time and adjust treatment targets as necessary, is also a critical piece of meaningful engagement. Additionally, bolstering multidisciplinary collaboration across systems is necessary so that families can feel as though they are a part of a coordinated team that has a shared understanding of the family's needs, strengths, and treatment goals.

FUTURE DIRECTIONS

While we accessed and used several important areas of literature and resources as we developed this book, we became increasingly aware of a few key areas that are deserving of more attention in the assessment literature. For example, the body of literature focused on meaningful and collaborative applications of assessment is quite limited; empirical studies that address these topics are also lacking. Furthermore, there are particularly few resources that are designed to help clinicians understand how to effectively and meaningfully engage and partner with families in the context of assessment and use assessment data as part of a collaborative service or treatment planning process.

Research is also needed to support our understanding of how comprehensive trauma-informed assessment can improve intervention practices and outcomes. For instance, empirical studies are needed to determine how the key components of an effective trauma-informed assessment process, as described in this book, might improve the process of delivering services to youth and families as well as outcomes related to mental health services. In this regard, clinicians would benefit from research that helps them understand how outcomes related to mental health treatment might improve if families were engaged more effectively from the outset of services, during the assessment phase. There also is a lack of research that reflects the actual experiences of people from different racial, ethnic, religious, and other cultural groups as they engage in trauma-informed assessment. These are topics deserving of more attention.

Another issue worth highlighting is that the recommendations included throughout this book are described in ways that most readily translate to an in-person trauma-informed assessment process; however, assessments can also take place when clinicians and families are unable to meet in person. For instance, advances in technology over the past decade have led to innovations in the field of mental health, including the provision of virtual mental health services. Accessing mental health services virtually (e.g., using a web-based platform) has allowed some individuals and families to access services when they may not otherwise have been able to do so. These virtual services may be of particular benefit to people who find it difficult to present to a clinic for care (e.g., people with significant physical disabilities, those with limited transportation options, those who live in remote locations relative to providers).

There has been a much greater focus on and demand for the delivery of virtual mental health services in the recent past during the COVID-19 pandemic. Enhancing a focus on virtual services can be of great benefit when organizations need to limit access to their physical space and in-person services in order to protect the safety of both their staff and their clients. It is critical that clinicians learn to competently and ethically provide virtual mental health treatment, including trauma-informed assessments. Many of the recommendations included in this book can be applied in virtual settings, but certain adaptations or adjustments may be required in order to maximize their effectiveness. We point readers toward a tip sheet on telemental health included as a resource in Appendix B of this book for further information on how to effectively conduct trauma-informed assessments virtually.

To our knowledge, this book is one of the first publications in the literature in which the linkage between psychological safety and the trauma-informed assessment process is explicitly stated. Future researchers and clinicians could benefit from diving more deeply into this process to identify specific mechanisms that enhance psychological safety in the assessment process. Furthermore, the current book highlights multiple types of tools that exist to support the trauma-informed assessment process. Yet based on our review, there is no existing resource to assist clinicians or agencies in selecting the tools that would best benefit the populations they serve in a structured and organized way.

Many professionals will likely experience some discomfort when conducting a trauma-informed assessment, whether virtually or in person, in part because it requires that they speak openly with youth and families about sensitive topics, such as their personal history of trauma and loss exposure. This potential discomfort is a reality that deserves acknowledgment; however, it is critical that providers engage in this work based on the sheer prevalence of trauma exposure among children and youth (e.g., those who seek mental health treatment, those in child welfare and juvenile justice settings). For this reason alone, we argue that all clinicians and mental health agencies (regardless of whether trauma-focused or more general in nature) actively work to increase both their comfort and their skills by incorporating at least some of the suggested trauma-informed assessment practices described in this book. Moreover, it is essential that both graduate and clinical training programs incorporate a focus on the trauma-informed assessment process and the meaningful applications of assessments in practice with youth and families. This focus would allow clinicians who engage in assessments and other aspects of clinical work with youth to increase their comfort level and develop skills in discussing sensitive trauma-related topics and sharing assessment findings in meaningful ways with families.

We hope this book will inspire others to view trauma-informed assessment, as well as other types of assessment, as an integral part of the treatment intervention process. If students and providers in training begin to see assessment as one of the first key steps of clinical practice and as a required piece of effective treatment, we may see an increase in the number of professionals who incorporate screening and assessment as a normal and integrated aspect of their work with all children and families. The regular use and application of assessments (both trauma-informed and more general in nature) within clinical settings creates opportunities for developing a shared understanding and increased transparency regarding the youths' and families' needs and strengths and the goals of treatment. We believe this practice will also enhance treatment and service delivery by objectively tracking treatment progress in a more standardized way over time.

In closing, we anticipate that the field of trauma-informed assessment will continue to evolve in relation to further research and the practice of dedicated and innovative clinicians. We are optimistic that this book will contribute to best practice with the wide range of concrete recommendations offered for clinicians who conduct trauma-informed assessments with children and families. We also strongly encourage ongoing and needed empirical work in this area, with an emphasis on further understanding how the essential process elements and structural components of assessment, as well as the engagement of families and translation of assessment information with families, can support better services overall and improved treatment outcomes for youth and families. We are hopeful that many clinicians will find this a useful resource as they practically apply a variety of the techniques and recommendations highlighted throughout this book.

Appendix A

ADDITIONAL RESOURCES

TRAUMA-INFORMED ASSESSMENT TOOLS

Measure reviews database: National Child Traumatic Stress Network
https://www.nctsn.org/treatments-and-practices/screening-and-assessments/measure-reviews

Measurement tools: California Evidence-Based Clearinghouse
for Child Welfare
https://www.cebc4cw.org/assessment-tools/measurement-tools/

Complex trauma standardized measures: National Child Traumatic
Stress Network
https://www.nctsn.org/resources/complex-trauma-standardized-measures

Adverse childhood experiences tools: ACEs Connection
https://www.acesconnection.com/g/resource-center/blog/resource-list-extended-aces-surveys

DEVELOPMENTAL ASSESSMENT TOOLS

Developmental assessment: Science Direct—Information on developmental
screening and assessment tools and their uses
https://www.sciencedirect.com/topics/psychology/developmental-assessment

Developmental monitoring and screening: Centers for Disease Control and
Prevention—Fact sheet highlighting differences among developmental
screening, monitoring, and evaluation
https://www.cdc.gov/ncbddd/childdevelopment/screening.html

Developmental screening and assessment: Zero to Three—Resources for developmental screening and assessment for young children
https://www.zerotothree.org/espanol/developmental-screening-and-assessment

Caregiver assessment tools: Family Caregiver Alliance
https://www.caregiver.org/sites/caregiver.org/files/pdfs/SelCGAssmtMeas_ResInv_FINAL_12.10.12.pdf

Tools to measure resilience, protective factors, and strengths: ACEs Connection
https://www.acesconnection.com/g/resource-center/blog/resource-list-resilience-surveys

Resources and surveys to support application of adverse childhood experiences tools: ACEs Connection
https://www.acesconnection.com/g/resource-center

TRAUMA COMPETENCIES

Guidelines on Trauma Competencies for Education and Training: American Psychological Association
https://www.apa.org/ed/resources/trauma-competencies-training.pdf

These guidelines include cross-cutting competencies, such as demonstrating the ability to appreciate and understand the impact of trauma on health outcomes and demonstrating knowledge of and understanding about trauma reactions and how to tailor trauma interventions and assessments in ways that honor and account for individual, cultural, community, and organizational diversity. In addition to these cross-cutting competencies, the guidelines reference the need to stay current regarding scientific knowledge, such as by demonstrating the ability to recognize the epidemiology of traumatic exposure outcomes and demonstrating an understanding of the social, historical, and cultural context in which trauma is experienced and researched. Additional content areas identified in these guidelines are psychological assessment, psychological intervention, professionalism, and relational systems. Readers are encouraged to review the document in its entirety and consider ways to ensure that they (as individual clinicians) or their staff (as agency leaders) meet these identified competencies.

Using the Secondary Traumatic Stress Core Competencies in Trauma-Informed Supervision: National Child Traumatic Stress Network
https://www.nctsn.org/resources/using-secondary-traumatic-stress-core-competencies-trauma-informed-supervision

The Secondary Traumatic Stress (STS) Core Competencies in trauma-informed supervision include the following:

1. knowledge of the signs, symptoms, and risk factors of STS and its impact on employees;

2. knowledge and capacity to self-assess, monitor, and address the supervisor's personal STS;

3. knowledge of how to encourage employees in sharing the emotional experience of doing trauma work in a safe and supportive manner;

4. skills to assist employees in emotional reregulation after difficult encounters;

5. knowledge of basic psychological first aid or other supportive approaches to assist staff after an emergency or crisis event;

6. ability to both model and coach supervisees in using a trauma lens to guide case conceptualization and service delivery;

7. knowledge of resilience factors and ability to structure resilience building into individual and group supervisory activities;

8. ability to distinguish between expected changes in supervisees' perspectives and cognitive distortions related to indirect trauma exposure; and

9. ability to use appropriate self-disclosure in supervisory sessions to enhance supervisees' ability to recognize, acknowledge, and respond to the impact of indirect trauma.

LGBTQ youth: National Child Traumatic Stress Network
https://www.nctsn.org/what-is-child-trauma/populations-at-risk/lgbtq-youth

The LGBTQ Youth page on the National Child Traumatic Stress Network website provides free access to 23 resources focused on working with sexual and gender minority youth in a trauma-informed way. Included are fact sheets, tip sheets, webinars, and videos to support service providers across a range of settings. Many of these resources can be helpful for youth and families as well.

Adverse Childhood Experiences (ACE) Study: Centers for Disease Control and Prevention
https://www.cdc.gov/violenceprevention/childabuseandneglect/acestudy/index.html

The Violence Prevention section of the Centers for Disease Control and Prevention website offers important information and background on the ACE Study. It includes several facts and findings from the ACE Study, major findings related to adverse childhood experiences across settings, applications of ACE Study data in practice, prevention strategies and prevention resources, and a range of other resources and tools.

Tip sheet, "Conducting Intakes and Assessments Using Telemental Health"—see Appendix B.

Appendix B

CONDUCTING INTAKES AND ASSESSMENTS USING TELEMENTAL HEALTH

With the emergence of COVID-19, multiple mental health providers have quickly transitioned from providing services face-to-face to providing those same services remotely via telehealth technology, such as Zoom. One of the more challenging aspects of this transition is moving the original intake and assessment process from an in-person encounter to a virtual one. The following guidance has been prepared to assist clinicians and offer suggested strategies and tips for conducting intakes and assessments via telemental health (TMH).

OVERVIEW OF THE TRAUMA-INFORMED MENTAL HEALTH ASSESSMENT PROCESS

The trauma-informed mental health assessment process is a multifaceted process that typically includes multiple techniques such as the following:

- a culturally sensitive and responsive clinical interview with the child and/or caregiver (which will vary based on the age of the child) in which the clinician collects information on the child's development, family history, exposure to trauma and loss, functioning across domains, other current challenges, and strengths;

- completion of standardized measures focused on general functioning and trauma-specific symptoms and needs;

- observation of the child and caregiver during the assessment process to gather information on nonverbal behaviors and interactions; and

- coordination with and gathering of information from other providers (e.g., teachers, caseworkers) and informants in the child's life to develop the general picture about the child's and family's functioning.

PREPARING THE CLIENT AND CAREGIVER FOR THE INTAKE AND ASSESSMENT PROCESS

- **Technology:** Discuss with the client and caregiver whether they have the adequate technology to engage in TMH. This technology may include a computer, a webcam, speakers, or a mobile device (such as a tablet or phone) that includes capacity for both video and audio.
  - Can you see me? Can you hear me?
  - Do we have any technology issues we need to address before we start?
  - If we get disconnected, I will call you back or resend a link to you so you do not need to worry about trying to recontact me.

- **Privacy:** Ensure that the child and caregiver have a private space for the assessment that is free from distractions and where they can answer questions freely. If they do not have a private space, suggest that they use headphones or ear buds.
  - Are you by yourself or with others right now? Do you have privacy?
  - Is it OK for you to talk about personal topics with me right now?
  - How are you and everyone in your family feeling [or doing]?

- **Transparency:** Discuss with the client that you are conducting the assessment via TMH, but that it is not ideal and might be a strange, new process for them. Be realistic and transparent about the challenges associated with collecting information in this way. Let them know that you will not give up on them, even if there are unforeseen challenges with the technology.

- **Safety:** As with any intake process, highlight safety and the need to maintain safety throughout the process. Know your risk assessment protocol.
  - Where are you? What is the address?
  - Who lives there with you? Who else is in your home right now?

- **Informed consent:** Make sure to complete the informed consent as soon as possible. It is recommended that you forward a copy of the informed consent to the family prior to the session so they have time to review it. During the first intake session, you can briefly review it and address any questions that may have emerged.

INITIAL TELEHEALTH SESSION PROTOCOL

- Obtain informed consent; discuss the consent form, including benefits, risks, and confidentiality.

- Get an emergency contact (besides the primary caregiver), including name, phone number, and address if possible.

- Discuss harm to self and duty to warn.

    - **Harm to self:** Let them know you will contact the parent, emergency contact, or 911 for them if you are worried about their immediate safety since you are not physically present.

    - **Duty to warn and mandated reporting:** Let them know that if you are worried about their immediate safety or the safety of others, you may have to involve and notify others to keep everyone safe.

- For younger children, let the caregiver know they will need to be present during the session to provide additional supervision if needed. For older youth, ask who else is home and discuss a plan of how to contact the caregiver if needed.

DEVELOPING TRUST AND RAPPORT

A key part of the assessment process is developing trust and rapport with the child and family so that they feel comfortable engaging in services and completing the assessment process. The development of trust and rapport begins with the child's and family's very first interaction with the provider. The following are some key strategies to help develop trust and rapport via TMH:

- Forward clients a welcome packet that describes your agency, and the services you provide, so that they can receive as much information as possible about who you are in advance.

- Begin the process of engagement by being transparent about how TMH is different from other forms of therapy, and acknowledge that this is likely a new experience for both therapists and clients. Share with the client that you will both be learning together and that you are committed to this process.

- Practice appropriate eye contact and body language. Keep your eyes on the camera you are using, rather than elsewhere on the screen, so the client will experience you as looking at them versus slightly away from them. Center yourself in front of your screen so that the child and caregiver can see you clearly.

- Ensure that your voice and tone are calm and connected. Over the course of a day conducting TMH sessions, you may get tired, slouch more often, and feel the need to speak more loudly, which can hurt your voice. Pay attention, and incorporate strategies to help maintain your voice as needed (e.g., lozenges, tea, voice exercises, good posture).

- During the initial interaction with the child and family, introduce yourself and describe your background and experience, how long you have been doing this work, and your qualifications. Provide the client with a sense of who you are and how you are equipped to help them.

- Create strategies to provide a virtual tour of the office so that the client can experience what it would be like to come into the office. This tour may be through photos shared with the client, or the therapist or intake assessor may take the client on a video tour of the space.

- Ask the child and caregiver to provide a tour of their own physical space—this may be their own room, the overall house, or a unique space they'd like to share with the therapist.

- At the end of the first session, check in with the client about the experience. What worked well for them? What was challenging? Do they want to continue with therapy? If so, what can be improved next time?

CONDUCTING THE CLINICAL INTERVIEW

During the course of the clinical interview, the therapist will ask the child and caregiver a number of deeply personal and detailed questions. For the therapist, asking these questions remotely can feel somewhat uncomfortable and impersonal. The following strategies can assist with the clinical interview process:

- Pay attention to body language as much as possible, given the use of technology (and its potential limitations).

- Expect the process of conducting an assessment via TMH to take longer than for a traditional assessment. Break up the time for conducting the assessment as much as possible to avoid fatigue for both you and the child and caregiver.

COMPLETION OF STANDARDIZED ASSESSMENT MEASURES

During a face-to-face assessment session, the therapist or intake assessor may provide the client and caregiver with assessment measures and ask them to complete them in the office before beginning the assessment sessions. However, this process may need to be adjusted during TMH as sending the measures to families to complete and send back can be time consuming and costly, particularly if the measures are misplaced. Therefore, the following adjustments can be made to the measure administration process:

- If a measure is available online and there is a confidential portal in which the child and caregiver can complete the measure privately, this is an option to consider.

- Otherwise, consider administering the measures verbally to the clients via TMH:

  - It can be helpful to scan a copy of the measure and share your screen so that the client can see the measure and follow along with the questions.

  - If that is not possible or it is difficult to see the measure, you can create a visual representation of just the scaling and share that document, asking the client and caregiver to provide ratings using the appropriate scaling for the measure.

  - As much as possible, provide the child and caregiver with options on how to complete the assessment. Do they want to read it quietly and just give responses? Do they want you to read the questions to them, and they then respond using a chat feature instead of out loud? If possible with the particular measure, does the client want you to fill in the answers on the form while you go through the questions together? Try to keep the process as engaging, interactive, and flexible as possible.

- Regardless, the therapist is encouraged to have a copy of the measure in front of them that they can fill in and then complete the scoring after the session is over.

- Alternatively, if there is a research assistant available to administer the measure via telehealth or over the telephone before the session using the above strategies (and if the caregiver and family are agreeable to this), this can be one way of minimizing time taken during the session to complete the measure.

PROVIDING FEEDBACK REGARDING THE ASSESSMENT RESULTS

A key part of the assessment process is sharing an overview of the assessment results with the family so that they can see how they rated compared with others on various items and understand their areas of strength and concern.

- Create an outline of all of the measures used and the types of information gathered in other ways (e.g., clinical interview with just the youth or caregiver, collateral contact with a teacher) so that the family can see at a glance where you received the information that you integrated and used to identify conclusions and recommendations.

- When sharing the results from the standardized measures, it can be helpful to scan any reports that are generated on the assessment results and share those in much the same way as you would during an in-person session.

References

Abram, K. M., Teplin, L. A., Charles, D. R., Longworth, S. L., McClelland, G. M., & Dulcan, M. K. (2004). Posttraumatic stress disorder and trauma in youth in juvenile detention. *Archives of General Psychiatry, 61*(4), 403–410. https://doi.org/10.1001/archpsyc.61.4.403

Achenbach, T. M., & Rescorla, L. A. (2001). *Manual for the ASEBA school-age forms & profiles.* University of Vermont, Research Center for Children, Youth, & Families.

Ackerman, P. T., Newton, J. E. O., McPherson, W. B., Jones, J. G., & Dykman, R. A. (1998). Prevalence of post traumatic stress disorder and other psychiatric diagnoses in three groups of abused children (sexual, physical, and both). *Child Abuse & Neglect, 22*(8), 759–774. https://doi.org/10.1016/S0145-2134(98)00062-3

Alegría, M., Fortuna, L. R., Lin, J. Y., Norris, F. H., Gao, S., Takeuchi, D. T., Jackson, J. S., Shrout, P. E., & Valentine, A. (2013). Prevalence, risk, and correlates of posttraumatic stress disorder across ethnic and racial minority groups in the United States. *Medical Care, 51*(12), 1114–1123. https://doi.org/10.1097/MLR.0000000000000007

American Academy of Child and Adolescent Psychiatry. (2010). Practice parameter for the assessment and treatment of children and adolescents with posttraumatic stress disorder. *Journal of the American Academy of Child and Adolescent Psychiatry, 49*(4), 414–430. https://doi.org/10.1016/j.jaac.2009.12.020

American Psychiatric Association. (1994). *Diagnostic and statistical manual of mental disorders* (4th ed.).

American Psychiatric Association. (2013). *Diagnostic and statistical manual of mental disorders* (5th ed.). https://doi.org/10.1176/appi.books.9780890425596

American Psychological Association. (2012). Guidelines for psychological practice with lesbian, gay, and bisexual clients. *American Psychologist, 67*(1), 10–42. https://doi.org/10.1037/a0024659

American Psychological Association. (2014). *APA guidelines for clinical supervision in health service psychology.* https://www.apa.org/about/policy/guidelines-supervision.pdf

American Psychological Association. (2015a). Guidelines for psychological practice with transgender and gender nonconforming people. *American Psychologist, 70*(9), 832–864. https://doi.org/10.1037/a0039906

American Psychological Association. (2015b). *Guidelines on trauma competencies for education and training.* https://www.apa.org/ed/resources/trauma-competencies-training.pdf

American Psychological Association. (2017). *Multicultural guidelines: An ecological approach to context, identity, and intersectionality, 2017.* https://www.apa.org/about/policy/multicultural-guidelines.pdf

American Psychological Association, Presidential Task Force on Posttraumatic Stress Disorder and Trauma in Children and Adolescents. (2018). *Children and trauma: Update for mental health professionals.* https://www.apa.org/pi/families/resources/update.pdf

American Psychological Association, Task Force on Immigration. (2013). *Working with immigrant-origin clients: An update for mental health professionals.* https://www.apa.org/topics/immigration/immigration-report-professionals.pdf

Armstrong, J. G., Putnam, F. W., Carlson, E. B., Libero, D. Z., & Smith, S. R. (1997). Development and validation of a measure of adolescent dissociation: The Adolescent Dissociative Experiences Scale. *Journal of Nervous and Mental Disease, 185*(8), 491–497. https://doi.org/10.1097/00005053-199708000-00003

Baglivio, M. T., Wolff, K. T., Piquero, A. R., Bilchik, S., Jackowski, K., Greenwald, M. A., & Epps, N. (2016). Maltreatment, child welfare, and recidivism in a sample of deep-end crossover youth. *Journal of Youth and Adolescence, 45,* 625–654. https://doi.org/10.1007/s10964-015-0407-9

Bailey, D. B., & Powell, T. (2005). Assessing the information needs of families in early intervention. In M. J. Guralnick (Ed.), *A developmental systems approach to early intervention: National and international perspectives* (pp. 151–183). Paul H. Brookes.

Berliner, L., & Elliott, D. M. (2002). Sexual abuse of children. In J. E. B. Myers, L. Berliner, J. Briere, C. T. Hendrix, C. Jenny, & T. A. Reid (Eds.), *The APSAC handbook on child maltreatment* (2nd ed., pp. 55–78). American Professional Society on the Abuse of Children.

Bickman, L., Kelley, S. D., Breda, C., de Andrade, A. R., & Riemer, M. (2011). Effects of routine feedback to clinicians on mental health outcomes of youths: Results of a randomized trial. *Psychiatric Services, 62*(12), 1423–1429. https://doi.org/10.1176/appi.ps.002052011

Black, M. C., Kresnow, M. J., Simon, T. R., Arias, I., & Shelley, G. (2006). Telephone survey respondents' reactions to questions regarding interpersonal violence. *Violence and Victims, 21*(4), 445–459. https://doi.org/10.1891/0886-6708.21.4.445

Blodgett, C., & Lanigan, J. D. (2018). The association between adverse childhood experience (ACE) and school success in elementary school children. *School Psychology Quarterly, 33*(1), 137–146. https://doi.org/10.1037/spq0000256

Bloom, S., & Farragher, B. (2014). *Restoring sanctuary: A new operating system for trauma-informed systems of care.* Oxford Press.

Boelen, P. A., & Smid, G. E. (2017). The Traumatic Grief Inventory Self-Report Version (TGI-SR): Introduction and preliminary psychometric evaluation. *Journal of Loss and Trauma, 22*(3), 196–212. https://doi.org/10.1080/15325024.2017.1284488

Boelen, P. A., Van Den Hout, M. A., & Van Den Bout, J. (2006). A cognitive–behavioral conceptualization of complicated grief. *Clinical Psychology: Science and Practice, 13*(2), 109–128. https://doi.org/10.1111/j.1468-2850.2006.00013.x

Boney-McCoy, S., & Finkelhor, D. (1995). Prior victimization: A risk factor for child sexual abuse and for PTSD-related symptomatology among sexually abused youth. *Child Abuse & Neglect, 19*(12), 1401–1421. https://doi.org/10.1016/0145-2134(95)00104-9

Borum, R., Bartel, P., & Forth, A. (2006). *Manual for the Structured Assessment of Violence Risk in Youth (SAVRY).* Psychological Assessment Resources.

Brewin, C. R., Rose, S., Andrews, B., Green, J., Tata, P., McEvedy, C., Turner, S., & Foa, E. B. (2002). Brief screening instrument for post-traumatic stress disorder. *The British Journal of Psychiatry, 181*(2), 158–162. https://doi.org/10.1192/bjp.181.2.158

Briere, J. (1995). *Trauma Symptom Inventory: Professional manual.* Psychological Assessment Resources.

Briere, J. (1996). *Trauma Symptom Checklist for Children (TSCC): Professional manual.* Psychological Assessment Resources.

Briere, J. (2001). *DAPS—Detailed Assessment of Posttraumatic Stress: Professional manual.* Psychological Assessment Resources.

Briere, J. (2005). *Trauma Symptom Checklist for Young Children (TSCYC): Professional manual.* Psychological Assessment Resources.

Briere, J., & Spinazzola, J. (2005). Phenomenology and psychological assessment of complex posttraumatic states. *Journal of Traumatic Stress, 18*(5), 401–412. https://doi.org/10.1002/jts.20048

Briere, J., & Spinazzola, J. (2009). Assessment of the sequelae of complex trauma. In C. Courtois & J. Ford (Eds.), *Treating complex traumatic stress disorders* (pp. 104–123). Guilford Press.

Briggs, E., Fairbank, J., Greeson, J., Layne, C. M., Steinberg, A. M., Amaya-Jackson, L. M., Ostrowski, S. A., Gerrity, E. T., Elmore, D. L., Belcher, H. M. E., & Pynoos, R. S. (2013). Links between child and adolescent trauma exposure and service use histories in a national clinic-referred sample. *Psychological Trauma: Theory, Research, Practice, and Policy, 5*(2), 101–109. https://doi.org/10.1037/a0027312

Bronfenbrenner, U. (1992). Ecological systems theory. In R. Vasta (Ed.), *Six theories of child development: Revised formulations and current issues* (pp. 187–249). Jessica Kingsley.

Carman, K. L., Dardess, P., Maurer, M., Sofaer, S., Adams, K., Bechtel, C., & Sweeney, J. (2013). Patient and family engagement: A framework for understanding the elements and developing interventions and policies. *Health Affairs, 32*(2), 223–231. https://doi.org/10.1377/hlthaff.2012.1133

Carter, R. T., Kirkinis, K., & Johnson, V. E. (2020). Relationships between trauma symptoms and race-based traumatic stress. *Traumatology, 26*(1), 11–18. https://doi.org/10.1037/trm0000217

Cashel, M. L. (2002). Child and adolescent psychological assessment: Current clinical practices and the impact of managed care. *Professional Psychology: Research and Practice, 33*(5), 446–453. https://doi.org/10.1037/0735-7028.33.5.446

Center for Child Trauma Assessment and Service Planning. (2014, July 10). *Caregiver focus group discussion for Illinois Department of Children and Family Services.*

Center for Child Trauma Assessment and Service Planning. (2015). *Use of the CANS in trauma-informed treatment and service planning.* http://cctasi.northwestern.edu/

Chadwick Center for Children and Families. (2009). *Assessment-based treatment for traumatized children: A Trauma Assessment Pathway (TAP).*

Chavez-Dueñas, N. Y., Adames, H. Y., Perez-Chavez, J. G., & Salas, S. P. (2019). Healing ethno-racial trauma in Latinx immigrant communities: Cultivating hope, resistance, and action. *American Psychologist, 74*(1), 49–62. https://doi.org/10.1037/amp0000289

Children's Bureau. (2018). *The AFCARS report.* U.S. Department of Health and Human Services. https://www.acf.hhs.gov/sites/default/files/cb/afcarsreport25.pdf

Child Welfare Information Gateway. (2016). *Family engagement: Partnering with families to improve child welfare outcomes.* U.S. Department of Health and Human Services, Children's Bureau.

Choi, K. R., & Graham-Bermann, S. A. (2018). Developmental considerations for assessment of trauma symptoms in preschoolers: A review of measures and diagnoses. *Journal of Child and Family Studies, 27*(11), 3427–3439. https://doi.org/10.1007/s10826-018-1177-2

Claussen, A. H., & Crittenden, P. M. (1991). Physical and psychological maltreatment: Relations among types of maltreatment. *Child Abuse & Neglect, 15*(1–2), 5–18. https://doi.org/10.1016/0145-2134(91)90085-R

Coates, S., & Gaensbauer, T. J. (2009). Event trauma in early childhood: Symptoms, assessment, intervention. *Child and Adolescent Psychiatric Clinics of North America, 18*(3), 611–626. https://doi.org/10.1016/j.chc.2009.03.005

Cohen, J. A., Mannarino, A. P., & Deblinger, E. (2006). Assessment strategies for traumatized children. In J. A. Cohen, A. P. Mannarino, & E. Deblinger (Eds.),

Treating trauma and traumatic grief in children and adolescents: A clinician's guide (pp. 20–31). Guilford Press.

Collins, K. S., Clarkson Freeman, P. A., Unick, G. J., Bellin, M. H., Reinicker, P., & Strieder, F. H. (2017). Child attributions mediate relationships between violence exposure and trauma symptomatology. *Advances in Social Work, 18*(1), 284–299. https://doi.org/10.18060/21283

Collins, K. S., Koeske, G. F., Russell, E. B., & Michalopoulos, L. M. (2013). Children's attributions of community violence exposure and trauma symptomatology. *Journal of Child & Adolescent Trauma, 6*, 201–216. https://doi.org/10.1080/19361521.2013.811458

Comas-Díaz, L., Hall, G. N., & Neville, H. A. (2019). Racial trauma: Theory, research, and healing: Introduction to the special issue. *American Psychologist, 74*(1), 1–5. https://doi.org/10.1037/amp0000442

Comas-Díaz, L., Hall, G. N., Neville, H. A., & Kazak, A. E. (Eds.). (2019). Racial trauma: Theory, research, and healing [Special issue]. *American Psychologist, 74*(1).

Conradi, L., Wherry, J., & Kisiel, C. (2011). Linking child welfare and mental health using trauma-informed screening and assessment practices. *Child Welfare, 90*(6), 129–147.

Cook, A., Spinazzola, J., Ford, J., Lanktree, C., Blaustein, M., Cloitre, M., DeRosa, R., Hubbard, R., Kagan, R., Liautaud, J., Mallah, K., Olafson, E., & van der Kolk, B. (2005). Complex trauma in children and adolescents. *Psychiatric Annals, 35*(5), 390–398. https://doi.org/10.3928/00485713-20050501-05

Cook, J. R., Hausman, E. M., Jensen-Doss, A., & Hawley, K. M. (2017). Assessment practices of child clinicians: Results from a national survey. *Assessment, 24*(2), 210–221. https://doi.org/10.1177/1073191115604353

Courtois, C. (2004). Complex trauma, complex reactions: Assessment and treatment. *Psychotherapy: Theory, Research, & Practice, 41*(4), 412–425. https://doi.org/10.1037/0033-3204.41.4.412

Cummings, N. A., & Cummings, J. L. (2008). Psychoeducation in conjunction with psychotherapy practice. In W. T. O'Donohue & N. A. Cummings (Eds.), *Evidence-based adjunctive treatments: Practical resources for the mental health professional* (pp. 41–59). Academic Press. https://doi.org/10.1016/B978-012088520-6.50004-4

Dalenberg, C. J., & Briere, J. (2017). Psychometric assessment of trauma. In S. N. Gold (Ed.), *APA handbook of trauma psychology* (Vol. 2, pp. 41–63). American Psychological Association. https://doi.org/10.1037/0000020-003

D'Andrea, W., Ford, J., Stolbach, B., Spinazzola, J., & van der Kolk, B. A. (2012). Understanding interpersonal trauma in children: Why we need a developmentally appropriate trauma diagnosis. *American Journal of Orthopsychiatry, 82*(2), 187–200. https://doi.org/10.1111/j.1939-0025.2012.01154.x

Darnell, D., Flaster, A., Hendricks, K., Kerbrat, A., & Comtois, K. A. (2019). Adolescent clinical populations and associations between trauma and behavioral and emotional problems. *Psychological Trauma: Theory, Research, Practice, and Policy, 11*(3), 266–273. https://doi.org/10.1037/tra0000371

D'Augelli, A. R. (2003). Lesbian and bisexual female youths aged 14 to 21: Developmental challenges and victimization experiences. *Journal of Lesbian Studies, 7*(4), 9–29. https://doi.org/10.1300/J155v07n04_02

de Arellano, M., & Danielson, C. K. (2008). Assessment of trauma history and trauma-related problems in ethnic minority child populations: An INFORMED approach. *Cognitive and Behavioral Practice, 15*(1), 53–66. https://doi.org/10.1016/j.cbpra.2006.09.008

De Bellis, M. D., & Zisk, A. (2014). The biological effects of childhood trauma. *Child and Adolescent Psychiatric Clinics of North America, 23*(2), 185–222, vii. https://doi.org/10.1016/j.chc.2014.01.002

Deblinger, E., & Runyon, M. K. (2005). Understanding and treating feelings of shame in children who have experienced maltreatment. *Child Maltreatment, 10*(4), 364–376. https://doi.org/10.1177/1077559505279306

Denton, R., Frogley, C., Jackson, S., John, M., & Querstret, D. (2017). The assessment of developmental trauma in children and adolescents: A review. *Clinical Child Psychology and Psychiatry, 22*(2), 260–287. https://doi.org/10.1177/1359104516631607

Dunn, C. (2018). *Trauma and individuals with intellectual and developmental disabilities: Tips and resources.* vkc.vumc.org/assets/files/tipsheets/traumatips.pdf

Enlow, M. B., Blood, E., & Egeland, B. (2013). Sociodemographic risk, developmental competence, and PTSD symptoms in young children exposed to interpersonal trauma in early life. *Journal of Traumatic Stress, 26*(6), 686–694. https://doi.org/10.1002/jts.21866

Falicov, C. J. (1988). Learning to think culturally. In H. A. Liddle, D. C. Breunlin, & R. C. Schwartz (Eds.), *Handbook of family therapy training and supervision* (pp. 335–357). Guilford Press.

Falicov, C. J. (2007). Working with transnational immigrants: Expanding meanings of family, community, and culture. *Family Process, 46*(2), 157–171. https://doi.org/10.1111/j.1545-5300.2007.00201.x

Fallot, R. D., & Harris, M. (2001). A trauma-informed approach to screening and assessment. In M. Harris & R. D. Fallot (Eds.), *Using trauma theory to design service systems* (New Directions for Mental Health Services No. 89, pp. 23–32). Jossey-Bass. https://doi.org/10.1002/yd.23320018904

Felitti, V. J., Anda, R. F., Nordenberg, D., Williamson, D. F., Spitz, A. M., Edwards, V., Koss, M. P., & Marks, J. S. (1998). Relationship of childhood abuse and household dysfunction to many of the leading causes of death in adults: The Adverse Childhood Experiences (ACE) Study. *American Journal of Preventive Medicine, 14*(4), 245–258. https://doi.org/10.1016/S0749-3797(98)00017-8

Figley, C. R. (1995). *Compassion fatigue: Coping with secondary traumatic stress disorder in those who treat the traumatized.* Brunner/Mazel.

Finello, K. M. (2011). Collaboration in the assessment and diagnosis of preschoolers: Challenges and opportunities. *Psychology in the Schools, 48*(5), 442–453. https://doi.org/10.1002/pits.20566

Finkelhor, D. (2018). Screening for adverse childhood experiences (ACEs): Cautions and suggestions. *Child Abuse & Neglect, 85,* 174–179. https://doi.org/10.1016/j.chiabu.2017.07.016

Finkelhor, D., & Berliner, L. (1995). Research on the treatment of sexually abused children: A review and recommendations. *Journal of the American Academy of Child & Adolescent Psychiatry, 34*(11), 1408–1423. https://doi.org/10.1097/00004583-199511000-00007

Finkelhor, D., Turner, H., Hamby, S., & Ormrod, R. (2011). *Polyvictimization: Children's exposure to multiple types of violence* [Juvenile Justice Bulletin No. 235504]. Office of Juvenile Justice and Delinquency Prevention.

Finkelhor, D., Vanderminden, J., Turner, H., Hamby, S., & Shattuck, A. (2014). Upset among youth in response to questions about exposure to violence, sexual assault and family maltreatment. *Child Abuse & Neglect, 38*(2), 217–223. https://doi.org/10.1016/j.chiabu.2013.07.021

Fisher, C. M., Woodford, M. R., Gartner, R. E., Sterzing, P. R., & Victor, B. G. (2019). Advancing research on LGBTQ microaggressions: A psychometric scoping review of measures. *Journal of Homosexuality, 66*(10), 1345–1379. https://doi.org/10.1080/00918369.2018.1539581

Foa, E. B., Johnson, K. M., Feeny, N. C., & Treadwell, K. R. H. (2001). The Child PTSD Symptom Scale: A preliminary examination of its psychometric properties. *Journal of Clinical Child Psychology, 30*(3), 376–384. https://doi.org/10.1207/S15374424JCCP3003_9

Foa, E. B., Keane, T. M., & Friedman, M. J. (2000). Guidelines for treatment of PTSD. *Journal of Traumatic Stress, 13*(4), 539–588. https://doi.org/10.1023/A:1007802031411

Fontes, L. A., & Plummer, C. (2010). Cultural issues in disclosures of child sexual abuse. *Journal of Child Sexual Abuse, 19*(5), 491–518. https://doi.org/10.1080/10538712.2010.512520

Ford, J. (2011). Assessing child and adolescent complex traumatic stress reactions. *Journal of Child and Adolescent Trauma, 4,* 217–232. https://doi.org/10.1080/19361521.2011.597080

Ford, J. D., Spinazzola, J., van der Kolk, B., & Grasso, D. J. (2018). Toward an empirically based developmental trauma disorder diagnosis for children: Factor structure, item characteristics, reliability, and validity of the Developmental Trauma Disorder Semi-Structured Interview. *Journal of Clinical Psychiatry, 79*(5), 17m11675. https://doi.org/10.4088/jcp.17m11675

Fox, N. A., & Leavitt, L. A. (1995). *The Violence Exposure Scale for Children–Revised (VEX-R).* Department of Human Development, University of Maryland.

Friedrich, W. N. (1997). *Child Sexual Behavior Inventory: Professional manual*. Psychological Assessment Resources.

Gadeberg, A. K., Montgomery, E., Frederiksen, H. W., & Norredam, M. (2017). Assessing trauma and mental health in refugee children and youth: A systematic review of validated screening and measurement tools. *European Journal of Public Health, 27*(3), 439–446. https://doi.org/10.1093/eurpub/ckx034

Gadeberg, A. K., & Norredam, M. (2016). Urgent need for validated trauma and mental health screening tools for refugee children and youth. *European Child & Adolescent Psychiatry, 25*, 929–931. https://doi.org/10.1007/s00787-016-0837-2

Gerson, R., & Rappaport, N. (2013). Traumatic stress and posttraumatic stress disorder in youth: Recent research findings on clinical impact, assessment, and treatment. *Journal of Adolescent Health, 52*(2), 137–143. https://doi.org/10.1016/j.jadohealth.2012.06.018

Ghosh-Ippen, C. G., Ford, J., Racusin, R., Acker, M., Bosquet, M., Rogers, K., Ellis, C., Schiffman, J., Ribbe, D., Cone, P., Lukovitz, M., & Edwards, J. (2002). *Traumatic Events Screening Inventory–Parent Report Revised*. Child Trauma Research Project of the Early Trauma Network and National Center for PTSD Dartmouth Child Trauma Research Group.

Goldsmith, R. E., Martin, C. G., & Smith, C. P. (2014). Systemic trauma. *Journal of Trauma & Dissociation, 15*(2), 117–132. https://doi.org/10.1080/15299732.2014.871666

Gomby, D. S. (2000). Promise and limitations of home visitation. *JAMA, 284*(11), 1430–1431. https://doi.org/10.1001/jama.284.11.1430

Gomes-Schwartz, J. M., Horowitz, J. M., Cardarelli, A. P., & Sauzier, M. (1990). The aftermath of child sexual abuse: 18 months later. In J. M. Gomes-Schwartz, J. M. Horowitz, & A. P. Cardarelli (Eds.), *Child sexual abuse: The initial effects* (pp. 132–152). Sage.

Gonzalez, A., Monzon, N., Solis, D., Jaycox, L., & Langley, A. K. (2016). Trauma exposure in elementary school children: Description of screening procedures, level of exposure, and posttraumatic stress symptoms. *School Mental Health, 8*(1), 77–88. https://doi.org/10.1007/s12310-015-9167-7

Gopalan, G., Goldstein, L., Klingenstein, K., Sicher, C., Blake, C., & McKay, M. M. (2010). Engaging families into child mental health treatment: Updates and special considerations. *Journal of the Canadian Academy of Child and Adolescent Psychiatry, 19*(3), 182–196.

Gothard, S., Ryan, B., & Heinrich, T. (2000). Treatment outcome for a maltreated population: Benefits, procedural decisions, and challenges. *Child Abuse & Neglect, 24*(8), 1037–1045. https://doi.org/10.1016/S0145-2134(00)00162-9

Grasso, D. J., Ford, J. D., & Briggs-Gowan, M. J. (2013). Early life trauma exposure and stress sensitivity in young children. *Journal of Pediatric Psychology, 38*(1), 94–103. https://doi.org/10.1093/jpepsy/jss101

Greenwald, R., & Rubin, A. (1999). Brief assessment of children's post-traumatic symptoms: Development and preliminary validation of parent and child scales. *Research on Social Work Practice, 9*(1), 61–75. https://doi.org/10.1177/104973159900900105

Greeson, J., Briggs-King, E., Kisiel, C., Layne, C. M., Ake, G. T., Ko, S., Gerrity, E., Steinberg, A., Pynoos, R., Howard, M. L., Pynoos, R. S., & Fairbank, J. (2011). Complex trauma and mental health in children and adolescents placed in foster care: Findings from the National Child Traumatic Stress Network. *Child Welfare, 90*(6), 91–108.

Griffin, G., Martinovich, Z., Gawron, T., & Lyons, J. S. (2009). Strengths moderate the impact of trauma on risk behaviors in child welfare. *Residential Treatment for Children & Youth, 26*(2), 105–118. https://doi.org/10.1080/08865710902872994

Guendelman, S., Medeiros, S., & Rampes, H. (2017). Mindfulness and emotion regulation: Insights from neurobiological, psychological, and clinical studies. *Frontiers in Psychology, 8*, 220. https://doi.org/10.3389/fpsyg.2017.00220

Habib, M., & Labruna, V. (2011). Clinical considerations in assessing trauma and PTSD in adolescents. *Journal of Child & Adolescent Trauma, 4*(3), 198–216. https://doi.org/10.1080/19361521.2011.597684

Habib, M., Sonnenklar, J., Labruna, V., Sunday, S., DeRosa, R., & Pelcovitz, D. (2005). *Structured Interview for Disorders of Extreme Stress–Adolescent Version (SIDES–A)*. North Shore University Hospital.

Hamada, R. S., Kameoka, V., Yanagida, E., & Chemtob, C. M. (2003). Assessment of elementary school children for disaster-related posttraumatic stress disorder symptoms: The Kauai Recovery Index. *Journal of Nervous and Mental Disease, 191*(4), 268–272. https://doi.org/10.1097/01.NMD.0000061147.39051.91

Hamby, S., Finkelhor, D., Turner, H., & Kracke, K. (2011). *The Juvenile Victimization Questionnaire toolkit.* https://www.unh.edu/ccrc/jvq/index_new.html

Hanson, T. C., Hesselbrock, M., Tworkowski, S. H., & Swan, S. (2002). The prevalence and management of trauma in the public domain: An agency and clinician perspective. *The Journal of Behavioral Health Services & Research, 29*(4), 365–380. https://doi.org/10.1007/BF02287344

Harris, M., & Fallot, R. (Eds.). (2001). *Using trauma theory to design service systems: New directions for mental health services*. Jossey-Bass.

Hatton, C., & Emerson, E. (2004). The relationship between life events and psychopathology amongst children with intellectual disabilities. *Journal of Applied Research in Intellectual Disabilities, 17*(2), 109–117. https://doi.org/10.1111/j.1360-2322.2004.00188.x

Hawkins, S. S., & Radcliffe, J. (2006). Current measures of PTSD for children and adolescents. *Journal of Pediatric Psychology, 31*(4), 420–430. https://doi.org/10.1093/jpepsy/jsj039

Hawley, K. M., & Weisz, J. R. (2005). Youth versus parent working alliance in usual clinical care: Distinctive associations with retention, satisfaction, and treatment outcome. *Journal of Clinical Child and Adolescent Psychology, 34*(1), 117–128. https://doi.org/10.1207/s15374424jccp3401_11

Hays, P. A. (1996). Addressing the complexities of culture and gender in counseling. *Journal of Counseling and Development, 74*(4), 332–338. https://doi.org/10.1002/j.1556-6676.1996.tb01876.x

Hays, P. A. (2008). Sorting things out: Culturally responsive assessment. In P. A. Hays (Ed.), *Addressing cultural complexities in practice* (2nd ed., pp. 105–127). American Psychological Association.

Hays, P. A. (2016). *Addressing cultural complexities in practice: Assessment, diagnosis, and therapy* (3rd ed.). American Psychological Association. https://doi.org/10.1037/14801-000

Herman, J. L. (1992). Complex PTSD: A syndrome in survivors of prolonged and repeated trauma. *Journal of Traumatic Stress, 5*(3), 377–391. https://doi.org/10.1002/jts.2490050305

Hodgdon, H. B., Spinazzola, J., Briggs, E. C., Liang, L. J., Steinberg, A. M., & Layne, C. M. (2018). Maltreatment type, exposure characteristics, and mental health outcomes among clinic referred trauma-exposed youth. *Child Abuse & Neglect, 82*, 12–22. https://doi.org/10.1016/j.chiabu.2018.05.021

Hopper, E. K., Bassuk, E. L., & Olivet, J. (2010). Shelter from the storm: Trauma-informed care in homelessness service settings. *The Open Health Services and Policy Journal, 3*, 80–100. https://doi.org/10.2174/1874924001003020080

Hunsley, J., & Mash, E. J. (2007). Evidence-based assessment. *Annual Review of Clinical Psychology, 3*, 29–51. https://doi.org/10.1146/annurev.clinpsy.3.022806.091419

Ingoldsby, E. M. (2010). Review of interventions to improve family engagement and retention in parent and child mental health programs. *Journal of Child and Family Studies, 19*(5), 629–645. https://doi.org/10.1007/s10826-009-9350-2

Ionita, G., & Fitzpatrick, M. (2014). Bringing science to clinical practice: A Canadian survey of psychological practice and usage of progress monitoring measures. *Canadian Psychology/Psychologie canadienne, 55*(3), 187–196. https://doi.org/10.1037/a0037355

Jensen-Doss, A., & Weisz, J. R. (2008). Diagnostic agreement predicts treatment process and outcomes in youth mental health clinics. *Journal of Consulting and Clinical Psychology, 76*(5), 711–722. https://doi.org/10.1037/0022-006X.76.5.711

The John Praed Foundation. (2015). *Transformational Collaborative Outcomes Management (TCOM)*. https://praedfoundation.org/tools/transformational-collaborative-outcomes-management-tcom/

Jones, R. E., Leen-Feldner, E. W., Olatunji, B. O., Reardon, L. E., & Hawks, E. (2009). Psychometric properties of the Affect Intensity and Reactivity Measure adapted for youth (AIR-Y). *Psychological Assessment, 21*(2), 162–175. https://doi.org/10.1037/a0015358

Jones, R. T., Fletcher, K., & Ribbe, D. R. (2002). *Child's Reaction to Traumatic Events Scale–Revised (CRTES–R): A self-report traumatic stress measure*. Virginia Tech.

Kaslow, N. (2000). *Children's Attributional Style Questionnaire–Revised (CASQ–R)*. Emory University, Department of Psychiatry.

Kassam-Adams, N. (2006). The Acute Stress Checklist for Children (ASC–Kids): Development of a child self-report measure. *Journal of Traumatic Stress, 19*(1), 129–139. https://doi.org/10.1002/jts.20090

Kisiel, C., Blaustein, M. E., Fogler, J., Ellis, H., & Saxe, G. N. (2009). Treating children with traumatic experiences: Understanding and assessing needs and strengths. In J. S. Lyons & D. A. Weiner (Eds.), *Behavioral health care: Assessment, service planning, and total clinical outcomes management* (pp. 17.1–17.18). Civic Research Institute.

Kisiel, C., Conradi, L., Fehrenbach, T., Torgersen, E., & Briggs, E. C. (2014). Assessing the effects of trauma in children and adolescents in practice settings. *Child and Adolescent Psychiatric Clinics of North America, 23*(2), 223–242, vii. https://doi.org/10.1016/j.chc.2013.12.007

Kisiel, C., Fehrenbach, T., Small, L., & Lyons, J. S. (2009). Assessment of complex trauma exposure, responses, and service needs among children and adolescents in child welfare. *Journal of Child & Adolescent Trauma, 2*(3), 143–160. https://doi.org/10.1080/19361520903120467

Kisiel, C., Lyons, J. S., Blaustein, M., Fehrenbach, T., Griffin, G., Germain, J., Saxe, G., Ellis, H., Praed Foundation, & National Child Traumatic Stress Network. (2013). *Child and Adolescent Needs and Strengths (CANS) manual: The CANS–Trauma Comprehensive Version: A comprehensive information integration tool for children and adolescents exposed to traumatic events*. Praed Foundation and National Center for Child Traumatic Stress.

Kisiel, C., Patterson, N., Torgersen, L., den Dunnen, W., Villa, C., & Fehrenbach, T. (2018). Assessment of the complex effects of trauma across child serving settings: Measurement properties of the CANS–Trauma Comprehensive. *Children and Youth Services Review, 86*, 64–75. https://doi.org/10.1016/j.childyouth.2017.12.032

Kisiel, C., Summersett-Ringgold, F., Weil, L. E. G., & McClelland, G. M. (2017). Understanding strengths in relation to complex trauma and mental health symptoms within child welfare. *Journal of Child and Family Studies, 26*(2), 437–451. https://doi.org/10.1007/s10826-016-0569-4

Kisiel, C., Torgersen, E., Weil, L. E. G., & Fehrenbach, T. (2018). Use of a structured approach to assessment within child welfare: Applications of the Child and Adolescent Needs and Strengths–Trauma Comprehensive (CANS–Trauma). In V. C. Strand & G. Sprang (Eds.), *Trauma responsive child welfare systems* (pp. 105–126). Springer. https://doi.org/10.1007/978-3-319-64602-2_7

Kisiel, C. L., Fehrenbach, T., Torgersen, E., Stolbach, B., McClelland, G., Griffin, G., & Burkman, K. (2014). Constellations of interpersonal trauma and symptoms in child welfare: Implications for a developmental trauma framework. *Journal of Family Violence, 29*, 1–14. https://doi.org/10.1007/s10896-013-9559-0

Knight, L. A., & Sullivan, M. A. (2006). Preliminary development of a measure to assess children's trauma attributions. *Journal of Aggression, Maltreatment & Trauma, 13*(2), 65–78. https://doi.org/10.1300/J146v13n02_05

Ko, S. J., Ford, J. D., Kassam-Adams, N., Berkowitz, S., Wilson, C., Wong, M., Brymer, M. J., & Layne, C. M. (2008). Creating trauma-informed systems: Child welfare, education, first responders, health care, juvenile justice. *Professional Psychology, Research and Practice, 39*(4), 396–404. https://doi.org/10.1037/0735-7028.39.4.396

Kosciw, J. G., Greytak, E. A., Zongrone, A. D., Clark, C. M., & Truong, N. L. (2018). *The 2017 National School Climate Survey: The experiences of lesbian, gay, bisexual, transgender, and queer youth in our nation's schools.* GLSEN.

Kovacs, M. (1992). *Children's Depression Inventory.* Multi-Health Systems.

Kroes, G., Veerman, J. W., & De Bruyn, E. E. (2005). The impact of the Big Five personality traits on reports of child behavior problems by different informants. *Journal of Abnormal Child Psychology, 33*, 231–240. https://doi.org/10.1007/s10802-005-1830-2

Lambert, M. J., Harmon, C., Slade, K., Whipple, J. L., & Hawkins, E. J. (2005). Providing feedback to psychotherapists on their patients' progress: Clinical results and practice suggestions. *Journal of Clinical Psychology, 61*(2), 165–174. https://doi.org/10.1002/jclp.20113

Lang, J. M., Ake, G., Barto, B., Caringi, J., Little, C., Baldwin, M. J., Sullivan, K., Tunno, A. M., Bodian, R., Stewart, C. J., Stevens, K., & Connell, C. M. (2017). Trauma screening in child welfare: Lessons learned from five states. *Journal of Child & Adolescent Trauma, 10*, 405–416. https://doi.org/10.1007/s40653-017-0155-y

Lanktree, C. B., & Briere, J. (1995). Outcome of therapy for sexually abused children: A repeated measures study. *Child Abuse & Neglect, 19*(9), 1145–1155. https://doi.org/10.1016/0145-2134(95)00075-J

Larsen, S. E., & Berenbaum, H. (2017). Did the *DSM-5* improve the traumatic stressor criterion? Association of *DSM-IV* and *DSM-5* Criterion A with posttraumatic stress disorder symptoms. *Psychopathology, 50*(6), 373–378. https://doi.org/10.1159/000481950

Layne, C. M., Kaplow, J. B., & Youngstrom, E. A. (2017). Applying evidence-based assessment to childhood trauma and bereavement: Concepts, principles, and practices. In M. A. Landolt, M. Cloitre, & U. Schnyder (Eds.), *Evidence-based treatments for trauma related disorders in children and adolescents* (pp. 67–96). Springer International. https://doi.org/10.1007/978-3-319-46138-0_4

Levendosky, A. A., Huth-Bocks, A. C., Semel, M. A., & Shapiro, D. L. (2002). Trauma symptoms in preschool-age children exposed to violence. *Journal of Interpersonal Violence, 17*(2), 150–164. https://doi.org/10.1177/0886260502017002003

Lyons, J. S. (2004). *Redressing the emperor: Improving our children's public mental health care system.* Praeger.

Lyons, J. S. (2009). *Communimetrics: A communication theory of measurement in human service settings*. Springer. https://doi.org/10.1007/978-0-387-92822-7

Lyons, J. S., & Israel, N. (2018, February 1). How TCOM takes person-centered care to scale. *TCOM Conversations*. https://tcomconversations.org/2018/02/01/how-tcom-takes-person-centered-care-to-scale/

Mahoney, K., Ford, J. D., Ko, S. J., & Siegfried, C. B. (2004). *Trauma-focused interventions for youth in the juvenile justice system*. National Child Traumatic Stress Network.

Mannarino, A. P., Cohen, J. A., & Berman, S. R. (1994). The Children's Attributions and Perceptions Scale: A new measure of sexual abuse-related factors. *Journal of Clinical Child Psychology*, *23*(2), 204–211. https://doi.org/10.1207/s15374424jccp2302_9

Masi, M. V., Miller, R. B., & Olson, M. M. (2003). Differences in dropout rates among individual, couple, and family therapy clients. *Contemporary Family Therapy*, *25*, 63–75. https://doi.org/10.1023/A:1022558021512

McCormick, A., Scheyd, K., & Terrazas, S. (2018). Trauma-informed care and LGBTQ youth: Considerations for advancing practice with youth with trauma experiences. *Families in Society*, *99*(2), 160–169. https://doi.org/10.1177/1044389418768550

McGee, R. A., Wolfe, D. A., & Wilson, S. K. (1997). Multiple maltreatment experiences and adolescent behavior problems: Adolescents' perspectives. *Development and Psychopathology*, *9*(1), 131–149. https://doi.org/10.1017/S0954579497001107

McKay, M. M., & Bannon, W. M., Jr. (2004). Engaging families in child mental health services. *Child and Adolescent Psychiatric Clinics of North America*, *13*(4), 905–921, vii. https://doi.org/10.1016/j.chc.2004.04.001

McKay, M. M., Hibbert, R., Hoagwood, K., Rodriguez, J., Murray, L., Legerski, J., & Fernandez, D. (2004). Integrating evidence-based engagement interventions into "real world" child mental health settings. *Brief Treatment and Crisis Intervention*, *4*(2), 177–186. https://doi.org/10.1093/brief-treatment/mhh014

Meehl, P. E. (1996). *Clinical versus statistical prediction: A theoretical analysis and a review of the evidence*. Jason Aronson. (Original work published 1954)

Mercer, B. L. (2011). Psychological assessment of children in a community mental health clinic. *Journal of Personality Assessment*, *93*(1), 1–6. https://doi.org/10.1080/00223891.2011.528741

Merino, Y., Adams, L., & Hall, W. J. (2018). Implicit bias and mental health professionals: Priorities and directions for research. *Psychiatric Services*, *69*(6), 723–725. https://doi.org/10.1176/appi.ps.201700294

Mevissen, L., Didden, R., Korzilius, H., & de Jongh, A. (2016). Assessing post-traumatic stress disorder in children with mild to borderline intellectual disabilities. *European Journal of Psychotraumatology*, *7*(1), 29786. https://doi.org/10.3402/ejpt.v7.29786

Miller, A. B., Hahn, E., Norona, C. R., Treves, S., St. Jean, N., Gassen Templet, L., McConnell, S., Chang, R., Abdi, S. M., & Ford-Paz, R. (2019). *A socio-culturally, linguistically-responsive, and trauma-informed approach to mental health interpretation*. National Center for Child Traumatic Stress.

Miller, A. B., Saxe, G., Stoddard, F., Bartholomew, D., Hall, E., Lopez, C., Kaplow, J. C., Koenen, K., Bosquet, M., & Reich, W. (2004, November 14–17). *Reliability and validity of the DICA-ASD* [Poster presentation]. International Society for Traumatic Stress Studies Annual Meeting, New Orleans, LA.

Milne, L., & Collin-Vezina, D. (2015). Assessment of children and youth in child protective services out-of-home care: An overview of trauma measures. *Psychology of Violence, 5*(2), 122–132. https://doi.org/10.1037/a0037865

Mohatt, N. V., Thompson, A. B., Thai, N. D., & Tebes, J. K. (2014). Historical trauma as public narrative: A conceptual review of how history impacts present-day health. *Social Science & Medicine, 106*, 128–136. https://doi.org/10.1016/j.socscimed.2014.01.043

Mooney, M. (2015). *Road to Recovery Toolkit, brief on early diagnosis*. https://learn.nctsn.org/mod/resource/view.php?id=11678

Mooney, M. (2017). Recognizing, treating, and preventing trauma in LGBTQ youth. *Journal of Family Strengths, 17*(2), 16. https://digitalcommons.library.tmc.edu/cgi/viewcontent.cgi?article=1363&context=jfs

Nadal, K. L., Whitman, C. N., Davis, L. S., Erazo, T., & Davidoff, K. C. (2016). Microaggressions toward lesbian, gay, bisexual, transgender, queer, and genderqueer people: A review of the literature. *Journal of Sex Research, 53*(4–5), 488–508. https://doi.org/10.1080/00224499.2016.1142495

Nader, K. (2007). Culture and the assessment of trauma in youths. In J. P. Wilson & C. S. Tang (Eds.), *Cross-cultural assessment of psychological trauma and PTSD* (pp. 169–196). Springer. https://doi.org/10.1007/978-0-387-70990-1_8

Nader, K. (2008a). Culture and family background. In K. Nader (Ed.), *Understanding and assessing trauma in children and adolescents: Measures, methods, and youth in context* (pp. 169–190). Routledge.

Nader, K. (2008b). *Understanding and assessing trauma in children and adolescents: Measures, methods and youth in context*. Routledge.

Nader, K. (2011). Trauma in children and adolescents: Issues related to age and complex traumatic reactions. *Journal of Child & Adolescent Trauma, 4*(3), 161–180. https://doi.org/10.1080/19361521.2011.597373

Nader, K. (Ed.). (2014). *Assessment of trauma in youths: Understanding issues of age, complexity, and associated variables*. Routledge.

Nader, K., & Salloum, A. (2011). Complicated grief reactions in children and adolescents. *Journal of Child & Adolescent Trauma, 4*(3), 233–257. https://doi.org/10.1080/19361521.2011.599358

National Child Traumatic Stress Network. (n.d.). *What is a traumatic event?* https://www.nctsn.org/what-is-child-trauma/about-child-trauma

National Child Traumatic Stress Network. (2004). *Facts on traumatic stress and children with developmental disabilities*. https://www.nctsn.org/sites/

default/files/resources//traumatic_stress_and_children_with_developmental_
disabilities.pdf

National Child Traumatic Stress Network. (2013, April). *Empowering therapists
to work with LGBTQ youth and families* [Webinar]. https://www.nctsn.org/
resources/empowering-therapists-work-lgbtq-youth-and-families

National Child Traumatic Stress Network. (2014, April). *Developing clinical
competence in working with LGBTQ youth and families* [Webinar]. https://
www.nctsn.org/resources/developing-clinical-competence-working-lgbtq-
youth-and-families

National Child Traumatic Stress Network. (2017). *Complex trauma: In juvenile
justice system involved youth.* https://www.nctsn.org/resources/complex-
trauma-juvenile-justice-system-involved-youth

National Child Traumatic Stress Network. (2019). *Select NCTSN resources related
to refugee and immigrant trauma.* https://www.nctsn.org/sites/default/files/
resources/fact-sheet/nctsn_resources_traumatic_separation_and_refugee_
and_immigrant_trauma.pdf

National Institute of Mental Health. (2001). *Blueprint for change: Research on
child and adolescent mental health.* National Advisory Mental Health Council
Workgroup on Child and Adolescent Mental Health Intervention Development and Deployment.

Newman, E. (2014). Assessment of PTSD and trauma exposure in adolescents.
In R. Greenwald (Ed.), *Trauma and juvenile delinquency: Theory, research, and
interventions* (pp. 59–77). Routledge.

Newman, E., Kaloupek, D. G., & Keane, T. M. (1996). Assessment of posttraumatic stress disorder in clinical and research settings. In B. A. van der
Kolk, A. C. McFarlane, & L. Weisaeth (Eds.), *Traumatic stress: The effects of
overwhelming experience on mind, body, and society* (pp. 242–275). Guilford
Press.

Office of Juvenile Justice and Delinquency Prevention. (2018). Delinquency cases
in juvenile court, 2014. *Juvenile Justice Statistics.* U.S. Department of Justice.
https://ojjdp.ojp.gov/sites/g/files/xyckuh176/files/pubs/251107.pdf

Ohan, J. L., Myers, K., & Collett, B. R. (2002). Ten-year review of rating
scales. IV: Scales assessing trauma and its effects. *Journal of the American
Academy of Child & Adolescent Psychiatry, 41*(12), 1401–1422. https://
doi.org/10.1097/00004583-200212000-00012

Oransky, M., Hahn, H., & Stover, C. S. (2013). Caregiver and youth agreement
regarding youths' trauma histories: Implications for youths' functioning
after exposure to trauma. *Journal of Youth and Adolescence, 42*, 1528–1542.
https://doi.org/10.1007/s10964-013-9947-z

Osterman, J. E., & de Jong, J. T. V. M. (2007). Cultural issues and trauma. In
M. J. Friedman, T. M. Keane, & P. A. Resick (Eds.), *Handbook of PTSD: Science
and practice* (pp. 425–446). Guilford Press.

Owen, J., Drinana, J. M., Tao, K. W., DasGupta, D. R., Zhang, Y. S., &
Adelson, J. (2018). An experimental test of microaggression detection in

psychotherapy: Therapist multicultural orientation. *Professional Psychology: Research and Practice, 49*(1), 9–21. https://doi.org/10.1037/pro0000152

Owen, J., Tao, K. W., Imel, Z. E., Wampold, B. E., & Rodolfa, E. (2014). Addressing racial and ethnic microaggressions in therapy. *Professional Psychology, Research and Practice, 45*(4), 283–290. https://doi.org/10.1037/a0037420

Pearlman, L. A. (2003). *Trauma and Attachment Belief Scale*. Western Psychological Services.

Pearlman, L. A., Wortman, C. B., Feuer, C. A., Farber, F. H., & Rando, T. A. (2014). *Treating traumatic bereavement*. Guilford Press.

Pelcovitz, D., van der Kolk, B., Roth, S., Mandel, F., Kaplan, S., & Resick, P. (1997). Development of a criteria set and a Structured Interview for Disorders of Extreme Stress (SIDES). *Journal of Traumatic Stress, 10*(1), 3–16. https://doi.org/10.1002/jts.2490100103

Perry, B. D., Pollard, R. A., Blakley, T. L., Baker, W. L., & Vigilante, D. (1995). Childhood trauma, the neurobiology of adaptation, and "use-dependent" development of the brain: How "states" become "traits." *Infant Mental Health Journal, 16*(4), 271–291. https://doi.org/10.1002/1097-0355(199524)16:4<271::AID-IMHJ2280160404>3.0.CO;2-B

Pfefferbaum, B., Jacobs, A. K., & Houston, J. B. (2012). Children and disasters: A framework for mental health assessment. *Journal of Emergency Management, 10*(5), 349–358. https://doi.org/10.5055/jem.2012.0112

Pfefferbaum, B., & North, C. S. (2013). Assessing children's disaster reactions and mental health needs: Screening and clinical evaluation. *Canadian Journal of Psychiatry, 58*(3), 135–142. https://doi.org/10.1177/070674371305800303

Pfefferbaum, B., & North, C. S. (2016). Child disaster mental health services: A review of the system of care, assessment approaches, and evidence base for intervention. *Current Psychiatry Reports, 18*, 5. https://doi.org/10.1007/s11920-015-0647-0

Prigerson, H. G., Horowitz, M. J., Jacobs, S. C., Parkes, C. M., Aslan, M., Goodkin, K., Raphael, B., Marwit, S. J., Wortman, C., Neimeyer, R. A., Bonanno, G. A., Block, S. D., Kissane, D., Boelen, P., Maercker, A., Litz, B. T., Johnson, J. G., First, M. B., & Maciejewski, P. K. (2009). Prolonged grief disorder: Psychometric validation of criteria proposed for *DSM-5* and *ICD-11*. *PLOS Medicine, 6*, e1000121. https://doi.org/10.1371/journal.pmed.1000121

Prins, A., Bovin, M. J., Kimerling, R., Kaloupek, D. G., Marx, B. P., Pless Kaiser, A., & Schnurr, P. P. (2015). *Primary Care PTSD Screen for DSM-5 (PC-PTSD-5)*. National Center for Posttraumatic Stress Disorder.

Putnam, F. W., Helmers, K., & Trickett, P. K. (1993). Development, reliability, and validity of a child dissociation scale. *Child Abuse & Neglect, 17*(6), 731–741. https://doi.org/10.1016/S0145-2134(08)80004-X

Pynoos, R. S., Weathers, F. W., Steinberg, A. M., Marx, B. P., Layne, C. M., Kaloupek, D. G., Schnurr, P. P., Keane, T. M., Blake, D. D., Newman, E., Nader, K. O., & Kriegler, J. A. (2015). *Clinician-Administered PTSD Scale for DSM-5–Child/Adolescent Version*. National Center for Posttraumatic Stress Disorder.

Quinn, A., Ji, P., & Nackerud, L. (2018). Predictors of secondary traumatic stress among social workers: Supervision, income, and caseload size. *Journal of Social Work, 19*(4), 504–528. https://doi.org/10.1177/1468017318762450

Quinn, M., Caldara, G., Collins, K., Owens, H., Ozodiegwu, I., Loudermilk, E., & Stinson, J. D. (2018). Methods for understanding childhood trauma: Modifying the Adverse Childhood Experiences International Questionnaire for cultural competency. *International Journal of Public Health, 63*, 149–151. https://doi.org/10.1007/s00038-017-1058-2

Roberts, A. L., Gilman, S. E., Breslau, J., Breslau, N., & Koenen, K. C. (2011). Race/ethnic differences in exposure to traumatic events, development of post-traumatic stress disorder, and treatment-seeking for post-traumatic stress disorder in the United States. *Psychological Medicine, 41*(1), 71–83. https://doi.org/10.1017/S0033291710000401

Roberts, A. L., Rosario, M., Corliss, H. L., Koenen, K. C., & Austin, S. B. (2012). Elevated risk of posttraumatic stress in sexual minority youths: Mediation by childhood abuse and gender nonconformity. *American Journal of Public Health, 102*(8), 1587–1593. https://doi.org/10.2105/AJPH.2011.300530

Rosado, L. M., & Shah, R. S. (2007, January). *Protecting youth from self-incrimination when undergoing screening, assessment and treatment within the juvenile justice system.* Juvenile Law Center. https://www.jlc.org/sites/default/files/publication_pdfs/protectingyouth.pdf

Rozzell, L. (2013). *The role of family engagement in creating trauma-informed juvenile justice systems.* National Child Traumatic Stress Network. https://www.nctsn.org/sites/default/files/resources//the_role_of_famiy_engagement_in_creating_trauma_informed_juvenile_justice_systems.pdf

Ryan, C., Russell, S. T., Huebner, D., Diaz, R., & Sanchez, J. (2010). Family acceptance in adolescence and the health of LGBT young adults. *Journal of Child and Adolescent Psychiatric Nursing, 23*(4), 205–213. https://doi.org/10.1111/j.1744-6171.2010.00246.x

Sacks, V., Murphey, D., & Moore, K. (2014). Adverse childhood experiences: National and state-level prevalence (Research Brief). *Child Trends.* https://www.childtrends.org/wp-content/uploads/2014/07/Brief-adverse-childhood-experiences_FINAL.pdf

Saigh, P. A. (2004). *A structured interview for diagnosing posttraumatic stress disorder: Children's PTSD Inventory.* PsychCorp.

Salston, M., & Figley, C. R. (2003). Secondary traumatic stress effects of working with survivors of criminal victimization. *Journal of Traumatic Stress, 16*(2), 167–174. https://doi.org/10.1023/A:1022899207206

Sampson, M., & Read, J. (2017). Are mental health staff getting better at asking about abuse and neglect? *International Journal of Mental Health Nursing, 26*(1), 95–104. https://doi.org/10.1111/inm.12237

Santiago-Rivera, A. L., Adames, H. Y., Chavez-Dueñas, N. Y., & Benson-Flórez, G. (2016). The impact of racism on communities of color: Historical contexts and contemporary issues. In A. N. Alvarez, C. T. H. Liang, & H. Neville (Eds.),

The cost of racism for people of color: Contextualizing experiences of discrimination (pp. 229–245). American Psychological Association. https://doi.org/10.1037/14852-011

Saylor, C. F., Swenson, C. C., Reynolds, S. S., & Taylor, M. (1999). The Pediatric Emotional Distress Scale: A brief screening measure for young children exposed to traumatic events. *Journal of Clinical Child Psychology, 28*(1), 70–81. https://doi.org/10.1207/s15374424jccp2801_6

Scheeringa, M. (2014). PTSD in children younger than the age of 13: Toward developmentally sensitive assessment and management. In K. Nader (Ed.), *Assessment of trauma in youths: Understanding issues of age, complexity, and associated variables* (pp. 21–37). Routledge.

Scheeringa, M. S., & Haslett, N. (2010). The reliability and criterion validity of the Diagnostic Infant and Preschool Assessment: A new diagnostic instrument for young children. *Child Psychiatry and Human Development, 41*(3), 299–312. https://doi.org/10.1007/s10578-009-0169-2

Scheeringa, M. S., & Zeanah, C. H. (1994). *PTSD Semi-Structured Interview and Observation Record for Infants and Young Children*. Department of Psychiatry and Neurology, Tulane University Health Sciences Center.

Scott, K., & Lewis, C. C. (2015). Using measurement-based care to enhance any treatment. *Cognitive and Behavioral Practice, 22*(1), 49–59. https://doi.org/10.1016/j.cbpra.2014.01.010

Secondary Traumatic Stress Committee. (2018). *Using the secondary traumatic stress core competencies in trauma-informed supervision*. National Child Traumatic Stress Network. https://www.nctsn.org/sites/default/files/resources/fact-sheet/using_the_secondary_traumatic_stress_core_competencies_in_trauma-informed_supervision.pdf

Seifert, K. (2007). *CARE2: Child and Adolescent Risk and Needs Evaluation Manual*. Acanthus.

Sibrava, N. J., Bjornsson, A. S., Pérez Benítez, A. C. I., Moitra, E., Weisberg, R. B., & Keller, M. B. (2019). Posttraumatic stress disorder in African American and Latinx adults: Clinical course and the role of racial and ethnic discrimination. *American Psychologist, 74*(1), 101–116. https://doi.org/10.1037/amp0000339

Simons, L., Schrager, S. M., Clark, L. F., Belzer, M., & Olson, J. (2013). Parental support and mental health among transgender adolescents. *The Journal of Adolescent Health, 53*(6), 791–793. https://doi.org/10.1016/j.jadohealth.2013.07.019

Smith, J. D. (2010). Therapeutic assessment with children and families: Current evidence and future directions. *Emotional & Behavioral Disorders in Youth, 10*(2), 39–43.

Snell-Johns, J., Mendez, J. L., & Smith, B. H. (2004). Evidence-based solutions for overcoming access barriers, decreasing attrition, and promoting change with underserved families. *Journal of Family Psychology, 18*(1), 19–35. https://doi.org/10.1037/0893-3200.18.1.19

Soto, A., Smith, T. B., Griner, D., Domenech Rodríguez, M., & Bernal, G. (2018). Cultural adaptations and therapist multicultural competence: Two meta-analytic reviews. *Journal of Clinical Psychology, 74*(11), 1907–1923. https://doi.org/10.1002/jclp.22679

Speier, A. (2006). Immediate needs assessment following catastrophic disaster incidents. In E. C. Ritchie, P. J. Watson, & M. J. Friedman (Eds.), *Interventions following mass violence and disasters* (pp. 80–99). Guilford Press.

Stein, B. D., Zima, B. T., Elliott, M. N., Burnam, M. A., Shahinfar, A., Fox, N. A., & Leavitt, L. A. (2001). Violence exposure among school-age children in foster care: Relationship to distress symptoms. *Journal of the American Academy of Child & Adolescent Psychiatry, 40*(5), 588–594. https://doi.org/10.1097/00004583-200105000-00019

Steinberg, A. M., Brymer, M. J., Decker, K. B., & Pynoos, R. S. (2004). The University of California at Los Angeles Post-Traumatic Stress Disorder Reaction Index. *Current Psychiatry Reports, 6*, 96–100. https://doi.org/10.1007/s11920-004-0048-2

Strand, V. C., Sarmiento, T. L., & Pasquale, L. E. (2005). Assessment and screening tools for trauma in children and adolescents: A review. *Trauma, Violence & Abuse, 6*(1), 55–78. https://doi.org/10.1177/1524838004272559

Substance Abuse and Mental Health Services Administration. (2014). *SAMHSA six key principles of trauma-informed approaches.* https://www.samhsa.gov/programs

Summersett Williams, F., Martinovich, Z., Kisiel, C., Griffin, G., Goldenthal, H., & Jordan, N. (2019). Can the development of protective factors help disrupt the foster care-to-prison pipeline? An examination of the association between justice system involvement and the development of youth protective factors. *Journal of Public Child Welfare.* Advance online publication. https://doi.org/10.1080/15548732.2019.1696912

Tawfik, S. H., Landoll, R. R., Blackwell, L. S., Taylor, C. J., & Hall, D. L. (2016). Supervision of clinical assessment: The Multilevel Assessment Supervision and Training (MAST) approach. *The Clinical Supervisor, 35*(1), 63–79. https://doi.org/10.1080/07325223.2016.1149751

Taylor, N., & Siegfried, C. (2005). *Helping children in the child welfare system heal from trauma: A systems integration approach.* National Center for Child Traumatic Stress.

Terr, L. C. (1991). Childhood traumas: An outline and overview. *The American Journal of Psychiatry, 148*(1), 10–20. https://doi.org/10.1176/ajp.148.1.10

Tharinger, D. J., Finn, S. E., Gentry, L., Hamilton, A., Fowler, J., Matson, M., Krumholz, L., & Walkowiak, J. (2009). Therapeutic assessment with children: A pilot study of treatment acceptability and outcome. *Journal of Personality Assessment, 91*(3), 238–244. https://doi.org/10.1080/00223890902794275

Tishelman, A., Haney, P., O'Brien, J., & Blaustein, M. (2010). A framework for school-based psychological evaluations: Utilizing a 'trauma lens.' *Journal of*

Child & Adolescent Trauma, *3*(4), 279–302. https://doi.org/10.1080/19361521.2010.523062

U.S. Census Bureau. (2018, February). *2016 National Survey of Children's Health: Methodology report.* U.S. Department of Commerce, Economic and Statistics Administration.

van der Kolk, B. (1998). Trauma and memory. *Psychiatry and Clinical Neurosciences*, *52*(Suppl. 1), S57–S69. https://doi.org/10.1046/j.1440-1819.1998.0520s5S97.x

van der Kolk, B., Ford, J. D., & Spinazzola, J. (2019). Comorbidity of developmental trauma disorder (DTD) and post-traumatic stress disorder: Findings from the DTD field trial. *European Journal of Psychotraumatology*, *10*(1), 1562841. https://doi.org/10.1080/20008198.2018.1562841

van der Kolk, B. A. (2005). Developmental trauma disorder: Toward a rational diagnosis for children with complex trauma histories. *Psychiatric Annals*, *35*(5), 401–408. https://doi.org/10.3928/00485713-20050501-06

van der Kolk, B. A., & Courtois, C. A. (2005). Editorial comments: Complex developmental trauma. *Journal of Traumatic Stress*, *18*(5), 385–388. https://doi.org/10.1002/jts.20046

van Os, E. C., Kalverboer, M. E., Zijlstra, A. E., Post, W. J., & Knorth, E. J. (2016). Knowledge of the unknown child: A systematic review of the elements of the best interests of the child assessment for recently arrived refugee children. *Clinical Child and Family Psychology Review*, *19*, 185–203. https://doi.org/10.1007/s10567-016-0209-y

Walls, M. L., & Whitbeck, L. B. (2011). Distress among Indigenous North Americans: Generalized and culturally relevant stressors. *Society and Mental Health*, *1*(2), 124–136. https://doi.org/10.1177/2156869311414919

Watson, S. D., Gomez, R., & Gullone, E. (2016). The Shame and Guilt scales of the Test of Self-Conscious Affect–Adolescent (TOSCA–A): Psychometric properties for responses from children, and measurement invariance across children and adolescents. *Frontiers in Psychology*, *7*, 635. https://doi.org/10.3389/fpsyg.2016.00635

Wigham, S., Hatton, C., & Taylor, J. L. (2011). The effects of traumatizing life events on people with intellectual disabilities: A systematic review. *Journal of Mental Health Research in Intellectual Disabilities*, *4*(1), 19–39. https://doi.org/10.1080/19315864.2010.534576

Williams, M., Printz, D. M. B., & DeLapp, R. C. T. (2018). Assessing racial trauma with the trauma symptoms of discrimination scale. *Psychology of Violence*, *8*(6), 735–747. https://doi.org/10.1037/vio0000212

World Health Organization. (2017). *Adverse Childhood Experiences International Questionnaire (ACE-IQ).* https://www.who.int/violence_injury_prevention/violence/activities/adverse_childhood_experiences/questionnaire.pdf?ua=1

Ybarra, M. L., Langhinrichsen-Rohling, J., Friend, J., & Diener-West, M. (2009). Impact of asking sensitive questions about violence to children and adolescents. *Journal of Adolescent Health*, *45*(5), 499–507. https://doi.org/10.1016/j.jadohealth.2009.03.009

Index

A

Abuse
  distress when asked about, 23–24
  increase in symptoms of sexually
    abused children, 29
  reluctance to disclose, 62
Acute Stress Checklist for Children, 98
ADDRESSING model, 83
Adolescent Dissociative Experiences Scale,
    90, 100
Adolescents. *See also* Youth
  author's use of term, 15
  identifying/assessing range of needs of, 6
  tailoring trauma-informed assessment
    to, 67, 69–71
  tools for assessment of, 90
Adverse childhood experience (ACE), 4–5
  ACE Checklist, 99
  Adverse Childhood Experiences
    International Questionnaire, 65
  Adverse Childhood Experiences (ACE)
    Study, 4, 41, 99
Adverse life experiences
  gathering information on, 41
  reviews of assessment tools for, 99
African Americans, PTSD in, 77, 78
Age, 67
  in ADDRESSING model, 83
  assessment across age groups, 106
  as consideration with young children,
    68–69
  and engagement of family in process, 109
  and selection of assessment tools, 89–94
American Academy of Child and
    Adolescent Psychiatry, 69

American Psychological Association
    (APA), 20
  guidelines for practice with LGBTQ
    clients, 76
  on psychological assessments, 83
  "supervision" defined by, 27
Applications of trauma-informed
    assessment, 107–118
  to bolster multidisciplinary collaboration
    across systems, 116–118
  family engagement in assessment
    process, 108–110. *See also* Core
    competencies
  future research needed on, 122–123
Assessment
  clinical setting general protocols for, 10
  evidence-based, 26–27, 105
  of mental health, 60
  screening vs., 6
  trauma-informed. *See* Trauma-informed
    assessment
Assessment translation, 108, 110, 113–116
Attributions about trauma
  defined, 44
  gathering information on, 39, 43–44
  reviews of assessment tools for, 102

B

Barriers
  in assessment of immigrant and refugee
    children, 80–81
  to effective assessment of trauma in
    young children, 68

intentional, 59–63
with system-involved youth and
families, 73–74
unintentional, 63–67
Behavioral observations, 51
Berliner, L., 29
Biases
among mental health clinicians, 79–80
regarding LGBTQ populations, 76
societal, 80
Black, M. C., 23
Boundaries, cultural, 62–63
Brain development, 99
Briere, J., 29, 42, 96–97

C

CANS (Child and Adolescent Needs and
Strengths)–Trauma Comprehensive
Version, 102, 104
Caregivers
author's use of term, 15
gathering information from, 49
needs and functioning of, 46–47.
See also Family and caregiver
needs and functioning
reports from, 98
strengths of, 47–48
trauma and loss history for, 46.
See also Family and caregiver
trauma and loss history
CBCL (Child Behavior Checklist), 90, 102
Child and Adolescent Needs and Strengths
(CANS)–Trauma Comprehensive
Version, 102, 104
Child and Adolescent Risk and Needs
Evaluation, 102
Child and Adolescent Version, 100
Child Behavior Checklist (CBCL), 90, 102
Child Dissociative Checklist, 91, 100
Children. See also Youth
author's use of term, 15
engaging, as active participants, 25–26
identifying/assessing needs of, 6
immigrant and refugee, 80–82. See also
Immigrant children
school-age, tools for assessment of, 90
self-report tools for, 86–87
strengths of, 47–48
young, tailoring trauma-informed
assessment to, 67–69
young, tools for use with, 89–90

Children's Attributional Style
Questionnaire–Revised, 102
Children's Attributions and Perceptions
Scale, 102
Children's PTSD Inventory, 100
Child self-report tools, 86–87
Child-serving settings. See also specific
settings
lack of information about youth trauma
history in, 10
tailoring assessment for youth and
families in, 72–74
trauma exposure in, 5
Child Sexual Behavior Inventory, 100
Child welfare system, 72–74
sharing information with, 117
tools for youth involved in, 97
youth of color and Indigenous heritage
in, 77–78
Choice, as key principle, 19
Chronic trauma
in child-serving settings, 5
tools for assessing, 90
Clients (term), 15
Clinical interviews
advantages and limits of, 50
recommendations for, 51
in telemental health, 134–135
Clinicians
author's use of term, 15
discomfort of, when asking about
experiences/symptoms, 23, 124
practical implementation strategies/
considerations for, 53–55
reluctance to incorporate tools by, 84
strategies to support well-being of, 24–25
supervision for, 27–28
training, 20–21
Coates, S., 68–69, 89
Collaboration
with families, ongoing, 116
in formulating treatment goals, 110
as key principle, 19
multidisciplinary, across systems,
116–118
with other providers, 50
terms used for, 107
when treating youth with intellectual
disabilities or developmental
disorders, 72
Collaborative treatment planning, 50,
113–116

Collins, K. S., 44
Collin-Vezina, D., 97
Communication
culturally mediated boundaries in,
62–63
for engaging family in process, 108
sharing information among providers,
116–118
styles and patterns of, 60
Community, strengths of, 47–48
Competencies. *See also* Core competencies
cultural, 58–59
trauma, 128–130
Complex trauma
in child-serving settings, 5
exposure, 41
as key information domain, 38
reactions, gathering information on, 43
reactions, reviews of assessment tools
for, 100–101
tools for youth involved with, 97
Complicated grief reactions
gathering information on, 45
as key information domain, 38
reviews of assessment tools for, 103
Comprehensive trauma-informed
assessment, 15. *See also* Trauma-
informed assessment
Conducting trauma-informed assessment,
training for, 20–21. *See also*
Implementing trauma-informed
assessment
Confidentiality
with adolescents' reporting, 70–71
discussing limits of, 62
when sharing information among
providers, 117
Conradi, L., 97
Contextual factors in selecting assessment
tools, 86–94
age and developmental considerations,
89–94
cultural considerations, 95
use of multiple informants and tool
formats, 86–88
Cook, J. R., 84
Core competencies
continuing to share progress and
collaborate with families, 116
explaining purpose of assessment, 111
of family engagement in assessment
process, 110–116

providing trauma-informed
psychoeducation, 111–112
resources on, 128–130
sharing results and facilitating
collaborative treatment planning,
113–116
for supervisors, 28
COVID-19, 123, 131
Cultural brokers, 63
Cultural competence, 58–59
Cultural considerations in selecting
assessment tools, 95
Cultural identity/preferences, 60
Cultural issues
as key principle, 19–20
valuing and responding sensitively to, 58.
See also Tailoring trauma-informed
assessment
Culturally relevant tools, 65, 66
Cultural values, 62–63, 66
Cumulative traumas, 66, 77

D

Dalenberg, C. J., 42
Danielson, C. K., 81–82
Darnell, D., 5
DD (developmental disorders), tailoring
trauma-informed assessment for, 71–72
De Arellano, M., 81–82
Demographic forms, 75
Denton, R., 97
Detailed Assessment of Posttraumatic
Stress, 104
*Developing Clinical Competence in Working
With LGBTQ Youth and Families*
(NCTSN), 76
Developmental assessment tools,
resources for, 127–128
Developmental disabilities, in
ADDRESSING model, 83
Developmental disorders (DD), tailoring
trauma-informed assessment for,
71–72
Developmental history
gathering/consolidating information
about, 36, 41–42
reviews of assessment tools for, 99
Developmental stage, 67
for adolescents, 69–71
and selection of assessment tools, 89–94
for young children, 68–69

Developmental trauma disorder, 101
Developmental Trauma Disorder
    Semi-Structured Interview, 101
Diagnoses
    challenges with, 52
    misdiagnosis, 4, 10, 52, 53, 55
    mislabeling, 4, 49, 52, 53, 55
    multiple, 48–49
    in young children, 68
Diagnostic and Statistical Manual of Mental
    Disorders (fifth ed., [DSM-5]), 53,
    66–68
Diagnostic assessment, 48–49
Diagnostic Infant and Preschool
    Assessment–PTSD scale, 90
Dialects of languages, 64
Disabilities, in ADDRESSING model, 83
Disaster responses
    assessments in context of, 88
    gathering information on, 45–46
    as key information domain, 38
    reviews of assessment tools for, 103
Disclosure, 62–63, 71
Discrepant information, 51–52, 87–88
Discrimination, 66
    as predictive of PTSD, 77, 78
    and racial trauma, 77
    self-reports of, for LGBTQ clients, 75–76
    against sexual and gender
        nonconforming youth, 74
Distress
    of clients, when asked about abuse
        and trauma, 23
    of clinician, getting support for, 25
Domains of trauma-informed assessment,
    39–48. See also individual domains
    adverse and stressful life experiences, 41
    developmental history, 36, 37, 41–42
    family and caregiver needs and
        functioning, 36–37, 46–47
    family and caregiver trauma and loss
        history, 36–37, 46
    reviews of assessment tools by, 98–104
    strengths of child, caregiver, and
        community, 37, 47–48
    tools specific to, 97–98
    trauma exposure and loss history, 36,
        37, 40–41
    trauma responses, 36, 37, 42–46
DSM-5 (Diagnostic and Statistical Manual
    of Mental Disorders, fifth ed.), 53,
    66–68

E

Education, trauma-informed, 111–112
Emotional responses to information, by
    clinician, 4–25
Emotional safety, 21
    creating environment of, 21–25
    strategies to promote, 22
Empowering Therapists to Work With LGBTQ
    Youth and Families (NCTSN), 76
Empowerment
    as key principle, 19
    through engagement of youth and
        family, 109, 111, 112
Engagement. See also Family engagement
    of child and family as active
        participants, 25–26
    of clinician in self-care, 25
    core competencies for, 110–116
    of family in assessment process,
        108–116
    and success of assessment process, 108
    of system-involved youth and families, 73
    use of term, 107
    of youth with intellectual disabilities or
        developmental disorders, 71
Essential (term), 15
Ethnic identity, in ADDRESSING model, 83
Ethnic minority clients
    disclosures for, 62
    diversity among, 80
    knowledge of historical events
        affecting, 67
    shared understanding of assessment
        process for, 61
    tailoring trauma-informed assessment to,
        76–80
Evidence-based assessment, 26
Evidence-based assessment tools, 26–27,
    105
Evidence-based processes, 26–27

F

Family
    deciding on key partners in, 109–110
    gathering information from, 49–50
Family and caregiver needs and
    functioning
    gathering information on, 46–47
    as key information domain, 39
    reviews of assessment tools for,
        103–104

Family and caregiver trauma and loss history
  gathering/consolidating information about, 36–37, 46
  as key information domain, 34, 39
  reviews of assessment tools for, 103–104
Family engagement, 7, 107–110, 122. *See also* Engagement
  engagement in assessment process by, 25–26, 108–116
Findings/results of assessment
  applying. *See* Applications of trauma-informed assessment
  explaining or translating, 11
  feedback on, in telemental health, 136
  sharing, 113–116
  for system-involved youth and families, 74
  when repeated over time, 29–30
Finkelhor, D., 29
Foster care system, 72
Four Rs of trauma-informed approach, 18
Functional difficulties
  defined, 102
  gathering information on, 43
  as key information domain, 38
  reviews of assessment tools for, 102

G

Gaensbauer, T. J., 68, 69, 89
Gender
  in ADDRESSING model, 83
  as key principle, 19–20
Gender minority youth, tailoring trauma-informed assessment to, 74–76
Generational influences, in ADDRESSING model, 83
Goal(s) of treatment
  engaging family in formulating, 110
  identifying needs and key issues to target as, 35
  involving family and youth in, 115
  symptom reduction as, 29
Gomes-Schwartz, J. M., 29
Grief reactions, 45. *See also* Complicated grief reactions
Grounding techniques, 24
"Guidelines for Psychological Practices With Transgender and Gender Nonconforming People" (APA), 76

"Guidelines for Psychological Practice With Lesbian, Gay, and Bisexual Clients" (APA), 76

H

Habib, M., 70
Harassment, of sexual and gender nonconforming youth, 74
Historical issues
  for immigrants or ethnic minority clients, 67
  as key principle, 19–20
Historical trauma
  defined, 77
  intergenerational, 77
  for people of color and Indigenous people, 76–80

I

ID (intellectual disabilities), tailoring trauma-informed assessment for, 71–72
Identity
  cultural, 60
  ethnic, 83
  racial, 83
  sexual, 74–76
Immigrant children
  cultural identity/preferences of, 60
  engaging important family members of, 110
  interpreters for, 63–64
  knowledge of historical events affecting, 67
  shared understanding of assessment process for, 61
  tailoring trauma-informed assessment to, 80–82
Implementing trauma-informed assessment, 33–55
  aspects of, 34
  assessing/understanding diagnoses, 48–49
  challenges in, 52–53
  gathering/consolidating assessment information, 36–39
  and key domains of trauma-informed assessment, 39–48
  with multiple reporters and range of assessment techniques, 49–52

practical strategies/considerations for clinicians, 53–55
structure and techniques for, 35–36
Indigenous heritage, in ADDRESSING model, 83
Indigenous people, tailoring trauma-informed assessment to, 76–80
Information
about strengths, 35
and communication styles/patterns, 60
confidentiality of, 62, 70–71, 117
consolidating and summarizing, 8
discrepant, 51–52, 87–88
gathering and consolidating, 36–39
key domains of, 34. *See also individual domains*
from multiple key adults in youth's life, 49–50, 65–66
sharing, 25–26, 35, 117
sociocultural variables in eliciting, 59
structure for understanding/interpreting, 34
Insular family dynamic, 62
Integrating evidence-based tools and processes, 26–27
Intellectual disabilities (ID), tailoring trauma-informed assessment for, 71–72
Intentional barriers
addressing, 59–63
boundaries, cultural values, and disclosure, 62–63
communication styles and patterns, 60
sensitive topics, 61
shared understanding of assessment process, 61–62
Interpreters, 63–64
Interventions
for engagement, 25
future research needed on, 123
psychoeducation to increase buy-in to, 112
Interviews
clinical, 50–51, 134–135
in telemental health, 134–135

J

Juvenile justice system
youth involved in, 72–74
youth of color and Indigenous heritage in, 77–78
Juvenile Victimization Questionnaire, 98

K

Kauai Recovery Index (KRI), 103
Key (term), 15
Kisiel, C., 97
KRI (Kauai Recovery Index), 103

L

Labruna, V., 70
Language
of assessment tools, 63–65, 94
fostering common language, 112
overcoming barriers of, 63–65
Lanktree, C. B., 29
Latinx people, PTSD in, 77, 78
LGBTQ youth, tailoring trauma-informed assessment to, 74–76
Loss history
of families and caregivers. *See* Family and caregiver trauma and loss history
gathering/consolidating information about, 36
of patients, 40–41
reviews of assessment tools for, 98

M

MBC (measurement-based care), 26
McKay, M. M., 25
Meaningful application of results, 107. *See also* Applications of trauma-informed assessment
Measurement-based care (MBC), 26
Mental health
assessing for diagnoses of, 48–49
communication styles/patterns in assessments of, 60
following trauma exposure, 102
terminology used for, 64–65
Mental health agencies
increasing comfort level and skills in, 124
tools for use in, 105
Mental health professionals/providers
assumptions and biases of, 79–80
author's use of term, 15
Mental health services, virtual, 123, 131–136
Mental health settings, 12
Microaggressions, 58–59, 66, 75–76
Milne, L., 97
Mindfulness, 24

Misdiagnosis, 4, 10, 52, 53, 55
Mislabeling, 4, 49, 52, 53, 55
Mooney, M., 76
Multidisciplinary collaboration across systems, 116–118
Multiple informants/reporters, 14, 49–52, 65, 86, 87
   gathering information from, 65–66
   tool formats for use with, 86–88
Mutuality, as key principle, 19

N

National Child Traumatic Stress Network (NCTSN), 4, 76, 82, 127, 129
   Secondary Traumatic Stress Committee of, 28
   webinars on working with LGBTQ youth and families, 76
   on work with immigrants and refugees, 82
National origin, in ADDRESSING model, 83
NCTSN. *See* National Child Traumatic Stress Network
Need(s)
   of family and caregiver. *See* Family and caregiver needs and functioning
   identifying areas of, 35–36
   of youth, identifying/assessing, 6
Negative cascade effect, 68

O

Observations, behavioral, 51
Ohan, J. L., 96
Organizational process elements, 18, 20–30. *See also* Process for trauma-informed assessment
   clinical supervision for support, 27–28
   creating safe environment, 21–25
   engaging child and family as active participants, 25–26
   integrating evidence-based tools and processes, 26–27
   as ongoing, 28–30
   training clinicians, 20–21
Orientation to assessment process, 53
Owen, J., 58

P

Patients (term), 15
Pediatric Emotional Distress Scale, 90

Pediatric medical settings, 89
Peer supervision, 27
Peer support, as key principle, 19
People of color (POC), tailoring trauma-informed assessment to, 76–80
Perceptions of trauma
   gathering information on, 43–44
   as key information domain, 39
   reviews of assessment tools for, 102
Physical safety, 21
   for LGBTQ youth and families, 75
   strategies to promote, 22
POC (people of color), tailoring trauma-informed assessment to, 76–80
Posttraumatic stress disorder (PTSD)
   accurate identification of, 68
   comorbidities with, 48, 104–106
   diagnosis of, 49
   in *DSM-5,* 66–68
   gathering information about, 42
   in people of color and Indigenous people, 77, 78
   and racial or historical trauma, 77
   in sexual and gender nonconforming youth, 74
   symptom manifestations of, 42, 43
   in youth with intellectual disabilities or developmental disorders, 71
Posttraumatic stress reactions
   gathering information about, 42
   reviews of assessment tools for, 100
Posttraumatic stress symptoms
   changes in expression of, 90
   cultural differences in expressing, 64
   and historical trauma, 77
   as key information domain, 37
   measuring presence of, 103
   wide range of, 105–106
Practice, future directions for, 122–125
Prejudiced behavior, among mental health clinicians, 79–80
Previous reviews of assessment tools, 96–98
Primary Care PTSD Screen for *DSM-5,* 103
Process for trauma-informed assessment, 7–8, 10–12, 119
   evidence-based, 26–27
   family engagement in, 108–116
   "ideal," 11, 52
   as ongoing, 54

organizational-level elements for.
    See Organizational process elements
orienting youth and family to, 53
with telemental health, 131–132
Professionals (term), 15
Progress, sharing, 116
Prolonged grief, 45
Protective factors, for sexual and gender
    nonconforming youth, 75
Providers. See also Clinicians
    author's use of term, 15
    education and training for, 11
    multidisciplinary collaboration across
        systems by, 116–118
    reports from, 98
Psychoeducation, trauma-informed, 49,
    111–112, 122
Psychological evaluation, 15
Psychological safety, 124
PTSD. See Posttraumatic stress disorder
PTSD in Preschool Aged Children scale,
    90, 100
PTSD Semi-Structured Interview and
    Observational Record, 100
Purpose of assessment, explaining, 111

Q

Questionnaires, 75

R

Racial identity, in ADDRESSING model,
    83
Racial minority clients
    diversity among, 80
    shared understanding of assessment
        process for, 61
    tailoring trauma-informed assessment
        to, 76–80
Racial trauma
    defined, 77
    differentiating reactions to, 78
    for people of color and Indigenous
        people, 76–80
Racism, 66, 77
Range of traumatic events, assessing for,
    66–67
Rapport
    and sociocultural factors, 60
    in telemental health, 133–134
Read, J., 23

Realizing impact of trauma and paths for
    recovery, 18
Reassessment, 7–8
    with adolescents, 70
    recommended frequency for, 29
    results from, 29–30
Recognizing signs/symptoms of trauma,
    18
Refugee children, tailoring trauma-
    informed assessment to, 80–82
Religion, in ADDRESSING model, 83
Reporters
    adolescents as, 69–70
    multiple, 49–52, 65–66, 86–88
Research, future directions for, 122–125
Resisting retraumatization, 18
Resources (for providers)
    on developmental assessment tools,
        127–128
    on tools for trauma-informed
        assessment, 127
    on trauma competencies, 128–130
Resources (of clients). See also Strengths
    in caregiver/family system and
        community, 48
    identifying specific areas of, 35, 37
Responding to assessments, 18
Responses to trauma, 4. See also Trauma
    responses
Results of assessments. See Findings/
    results of assessment
Retraumatization, resisting, 18
Reverse sleeper effect, 29
Reviews of assessment tools
    by domain, 98–104
    previous, 96–98
Rights of participants, 61–62
Risk behaviors
    in adolescents, 69
    gathering information on, 43
    as key information domain, 38
    in LGBTQ youth, 74–76
    reviews of assessment tools for, 102
Risk factors, assessing, 102

S

Safe environment
    clinical supervision as, 27
    creating, 21–25
    for LGBTQ youth and families, 75

Safety
  clinician's feeling of, 24
  creating environment of, 21–25
  emotional, 22
  as key principle, 19
  physical, 21, 22, 75
  psychological, 124
  and sociocultural factors, 60
SAMHSA (Substance Abuse and Mental
    Health Services Administration),
    17–20
Sampson, M., 23
School-age children, tools for assessment
    of, 90
School-based trauma-informed
    assessment, 88
Screening
  assessment vs., 6
  disaster, 45–46
  trauma, 10–11
Secondary Traumatic Stress Committee,
    National Child Traumatic Stress
    Network, 28
"Select NCTSN Resources Related to
    Refugee and Immigrant Trauma"
    (NCTSN), 82
Self-dysregulation, 43
Self-reports of discrimination, for LGBTQ
    clients, 75–76
Self-report tools
  child, 86–87
  Youth Self-Report, 90
Sensitive topics, cultural variability
    regarding, 61
Service providers, gathering information
    from, 50. *See also* Providers
Settings of assessment. *See also specific
    settings, e.g.:* Child-serving settings
  domains to include across, 97
  factors to consider across, 88–89
Sexual abuse
  and increase in symptoms of children, 29
  reluctance to disclose, 62
Sexual identity/orientation
  in ADDRESSING model, 83
  tailoring trauma-informed assessment
    to, 74–76
Sexual minority youth, tailoring trauma-
    informed assessment to, 74–76
Shame and Guilt scales, Test of
    Self-Conscious Affect–Adolescent,
    102

Shared understanding of assessment
    process
  from education about trauma, 112
  and sociocultural backgrounds, 61–62
Sibrava, N. J., 77
SIDES (Structured Interview for Disorders
    of Extreme Stress), 101
Societal biases, 80
Sociocultural context. *See also* Tailoring
    trauma-informed assessment
  defined, 57
  for experiencing/describing trauma-
    related symptoms, 64
  hierarchical structures in, 65–66
  understanding clients within, 59
  valuing and responding sensitively to, 58
Socioeconomic status, in ADDRESSING
    model, 83
Soto, A., 58–59
Spinazzola, J., 96–97
Spirituality, in ADDRESSING model, 83
Standardized assessment tools, 85, 97,
    105, 106, 135–136
Strand, V. C., 86, 96
Strengths (child, caregiver, and
    community). *See also* Resources
  gathering/consolidating information
    about, 37, 47–48
  identifying areas of, 35–36
  as key information domain, 39
  reviews of assessment tools for, 104
  of system-involved youth and families, 74
Stressful life experiences
  encouraging recall of, 66
  gathering information on, 41
  of refugee children, 81
  reviews of assessment tools for, 99
Structure. *See also* Process for trauma-
    informed assessment
  for information gathering and
    identifying/addressing needs, 7
  for trauma-informed assessment, 8–9,
    35–36
  for understanding and interpreting
    information, 34
Structured Assessment of Violence Risk in
    Youth, 102
Structured Interview for Disorders of
    Extreme Stress (SIDES), 101
Substance Abuse and Mental Health
    Services Administration (SAMHSA),
    17–20

Supervision
  APA definition of, 27
  for support in trauma-informed
    assessment, 27–28
Supervisors, core competencies for, 28
Symptoms of trauma. See also
    Posttraumatic stress symptoms
  adolescents' reporting of, 69–70
  changes in expression of, 90
  clinicians' discomfort with asking
    about, 23
  making connections among, 52
  of posttraumatic stress, 37, 42, 43, 64
  reduction of, as goal of treatment, 29
  sociocultural context for experiencing/
    describing, 64
Systemic traumas, 66
System-induced trauma, 73
System integration, 107
System-involved youth and families,
    tailoring trauma-informed
    assessment to, 72–74

T

Tailoring trauma-informed assessment,
    57–83
  addressing intentional barriers, 59–63
  addressing unintentional barriers,
    63–67
  for adolescents, 67, 69–71
  for immigrant and refugee children,
    80–82
  for LGBTQ and other sexual and gender
    minority youth, 74–76
  for people of color and indigenous
    people, 76–80
  for system-involved youth and families,
    72–74
  for young children, 67–69
  for youth with intellectual or
    developmental disabilities, 71–72
Teaming, 107
Techniques
  of assessment, using range of, 49–52.
    See also Tools for trauma-informed
    assessment
  for implementing trauma-informed
    assessment, 35–36
Telemental health (TMH), 131–136
  assessment process in, 131–132
  conducting clinical interview, 134–135

developing trust and rapport, 133–134
  feedback regarding assessment results
    in, 136
  initial session protocol, 133
  preparing client and caregiver for,
    132–133
Terminology, 15
Therapeutic alliance
  during assessment process, 109
  microaggressions negatively impacting,
    58–59
Therapists (term), 15
Time constraints for assessment, 53–54
TMH. See Telemental health
Tool (term), 15
Tools for trauma-informed assessment,
    10, 85–106
  challenges and practical considerations
    for clinicians, 104–106
  completed before sessions, 54
  contextual factors in selecting, 86–94
  culturally relevant, 65, 66
  evidence-based, 26–27, 105
  focused on racial or historical trauma, 79
  identifying relevance of, 54
  lack of consensus regarding, 68
  languages of, 63–65, 94
  previous reviews of, 96–98
  questions to consider when selecting,
    94, 95
  readministering core set of, 29
  resources for, 127–128
  review of, by domain, 98–104
  standardized, 85, 97, 105, 106,
    135–136
  and systemic/cumulative traumas, 66
  for use with immigrants and refugees,
    80–81
  using range of, 50
  in youth with intellectual disabilities
    or developmental disorders, 71
Training
  as organizational process element, 20–21
  for other staff, 55
  promoting staff/clinical training, 12–14,
    16, 18, 20, 23, 30–31, 83, 88, 95,
    124, 128
  to support making connections among
    symptoms, 52
Translation. See also Assessment
    translation
  assessment, 108, 110, 113–116
  interpreters for, 63–64

Transparency
  to create trust, 111
  as key principle, 19
Trauma(s). *See also specific topics*
  chronic, 5, 90
  complex, 5, 38, 41, 97
  cumulative, 66, 77
  distress when asked about, 23–24
  historical, 76–80
  racial, 76–80
  realizing impact of, 18
  systemic, 66
  system-induced, 73
  terminology used for, 64–65
Trauma exposure
  in child-serving settings, 5–6
  as domain of trauma-informed
    assessment, 40–41
  gathering/consolidating information
    about, 36
  mislabeling, misdiagnosis, or
    misunderstanding of impact of, 4
  prevalence of, 4, 5
  reviews of assessment tools for, 98
  for sexual and gender nonconforming
    youth, 74
  underrecognition of, 6
  young children's exposure to, 68
Trauma-informed assessment, 3–12,
    17–31. *See also specific topics, e.g.:*
    Implementing trauma-informed
    assessment
  anticipated evolution of, 125
  author's use of term, 15
  challenges and practical considerations
    with, 30
  conduct of, 7
  defined, 6–7
  framework for, 8–9, 119
  key issues and challenges with, 9–12
  key principles of, 18–20
  key recommendations for, 120–122
  need for more empirical evidence on, 53
  occurrence of, 7
  organizational process elements of,
    20–30
  process for, 7, 10–12
  psychological evaluation vs., 15
  range of needs identification/
    assessment in, 6
  reasons for not using, 10–11
  reassessment in, 7–8

  terminology used with, 15
  tools for, 10
Trauma-informed care, 5–6
Trauma-informed psychoeducation, 49,
    111–112, 122
Trauma responses
  complex trauma reactions, 43
  functional difficulties and risk
    behaviors, 43
  gathering/consolidating information
    about, 36, 42–46
  perceptions and attributions about
    trauma, 43–44
  posttraumatic stress reactions, 42
  reviews of assessment tools for,
    100–103
  subtypes of, 45–46
  trauma triggers or reminders, 44–46
Trauma screening
  defined, 6
  reasons for not using, 10–11
  universal approach to, 6
Trauma Screening Questionnaire, 103
Trauma Symptom Checklist for Children
    (TSCC), 90, 100
Trauma Symptom Checklist for Young
    Children (TSCYC), 90, 100
Trauma Symptom Inventory, 104
Traumatic event(s)
  adolescents' exposure to, 69
  around migration, 80
  assessing for broad range of, 66–67
  characteristics of, 40–41
  circumstances surrounding, 40
  defined, 4
  discrepant reports of, 88
  incorporating questions about, 66–67
  terminology used for, 64–65
  types of, 40
  witnessing of, 4
Traumatic Events Screening Inventory–
    Revised, 98
Traumatic grief, 45
Traumatic Grief Inventory, 103
Trauma triggers or reminders
  defined, 44
  gathering information on, 44–46
  as key information domain, 39
Trust
  with adolescents, 70
  during assessment process, 108, 109

with people of color, 78
in relation to cultural responsiveness, 59–60
with system-involved youth, 74, 76
in telemental health, 133–134
transparency for creation of, 111
Trustworthiness
as key principle, 19
and sociocultural factors, 60
TSCC (Trauma Symptom Checklist for Children), 90, 100
TSCYC (Trauma Symptom Checklist for Young Children), 90, 100

U

Unintentional barriers
addressing, 63–67
and assessing for broad range of traumatic events, 66–67
gathering information from multiple informants, 65–66
language barriers, 63–65
Universal screening, 6
Utility of comprehensive trauma-informed assessment, 35–36

V

Values, cultural, 62–63, 66
Violence Exposure Scale for Children–Revised, 98

Virtual mental health services, 123, 131–136
Voice, as key principle, 19

Y

Ybarra, M. L., 23–24
Young children
tailoring trauma-informed assessment to, 67–69
tools for use with, 89–90
Youth. *See also* Adolescents; Children
author's use of term, 15
challenges to trauma-informed screening/assessment with, 10–11
checking on areas of concern for, 54
in child-serving settings, trauma exposure for, 5
distress of, when asked about abuse and trauma, 23–24
with intellectual or developmental disabilities, 71–72
LGBTQ and other sexual and gender minority, 74–76
prevalence of trauma exposure among, 4, 5, 10
served in mental health settings, 12
Youth Self-Report, 90
Youth trauma history
lack of information about, in child-serving settings, 10
tools for assessing, 96–97

About the Authors

Cassandra Kisiel, PhD, is an associate professor and clinical psychologist in the Mental Health Services and Policy Program and the Department of Psychiatry and Behavioral Sciences at Northwestern University Feinberg School of Medicine. She serves as the principal investigator and director of the Center for Child Trauma Assessment, Services and Interventions, a center of The National Child Traumatic Stress Network (NCTSN) that specializes in the development of trauma-informed child-serving systems through training and support for these systems to recognize, understand, assess, and respond to the developmental effects of childhood trauma.

Dr. Kisiel is recognized as an expert in trauma-informed assessment within the NCTSN. She has more than 20 years of experience specializing in the complex developmental effects of trauma, with a focus on dissociation, strengths, and resilience; child trauma assessment; and evaluation. She has written and lectured extensively on the assessment and treatment and services for children exposed to complex trauma across child-serving settings. She also has extensive experience in supporting the implementation of trauma-informed practices, including a range of intervention approaches and assessment strategies with practitioners across the country.

Dr. Kisiel has specialized in the use of innovative training, implementation, and quality improvement approaches to support practice changes across various child-serving settings. This involved leading the initial adaptation and implementation of the Breakthrough Series Collaborative model for use within the child trauma field through her former role as training director for the National Center for Child Traumatic Stress at the University of California, Los Angeles. Dr. Kisiel is the primary developer of the Child and Adolescent Needs and Strengths (CANS)–Trauma version, including the most recent CANS–Trauma Comprehensive tool, developed in collaboration with the

NCTSN and with applications in numerous child-serving systems across the United States and in several other countries.

Tracy Fehrenbach, PhD, is a licensed clinical psychologist and assistant professor in the Mental Health Services and Policy Program at Northwestern University Feinberg School of Medicine. She serves as codirector and a coinvestigator for the Center for Child Trauma Assessment, Services and Interventions, a center of The National Child Traumatic Stress Network. As a clinician and researcher, she specializes in the impact of interpersonal trauma across the life span. More specifically, Dr. Fehrenbach is interested in maximizing the effectiveness of trauma-informed interventions through community–professional partnerships and by recognizing and building on personal and sociocultural strengths. She has published and lectured widely in these areas throughout the United States and Mexico and has a decade of experience supporting providers in their use of trauma-informed screening, assessment, and intervention in mental health, educational, child welfare, and juvenile justice settings.

Lisa Conradi, PsyD, is the director of clinical operations at the Chadwick Center for Children and Families at Rady Children's Hospital–San Diego, where she oversees all clinical programs at the Chadwick Center, a child advocacy center and one of the largest trauma treatment centers in the nation. Dr. Conradi has multiple years of experience in the field of child trauma and in supporting service systems to become more trauma informed. She has authored and coauthored a variety of publications on trauma screening and assessment practices and creation of trauma-informed systems, and she has presented nationally on innovative practices designed to improve the service delivery system for children who have experienced trauma. Dr. Conradi is one of the developers of the second edition of the *Child Welfare Trauma Training Toolkit* (NCTSN, 2013) and served as the project director for the Chadwick Trauma-Informed Systems Dissemination and Implementation Project, and she oversaw the development of multiple resources and materials designed to help systems become trauma informed. She also served as the program manager for the Breakthrough Series Collaborative on *Using Trauma-Informed Child Welfare Practice to Improve Placement Stability* (2012) under subcontract with the National Center for Child Traumatic Stress at the University of California, Los Angeles.

Lindsey Weil, PhD, is a clinical psychologist. She earned her PhD at Northwestern University and completed her postdoctoral fellowship at the

University of Washington. Dr. Weil also holds an MA in counseling psychology from Santa Clara University. Her current research focuses on health and well-being among youth in the child welfare and juvenile justice systems, placement stability and permanency, strengths and protective factors, and the meaningful use of trauma assessment. Her research has been funded by the American Psychological Foundation and the Doris Duke Fellowships for the Promotion of Child Well-Being.